ZECHARIAH

by
J. CARL LANEY

MOODY PRESS
CHICAGO

All Scripture quotations, unless noted otherwise, are from the *New American Standard
Bible,* © 1960, 1962, 1963, 1968, 1971, 1972, 1973, 1975, and 1977 by the Lockman
Foundation, and are used by permission.

Library of Congress Cataloging in Publication Data

Laney, J. Carl, 1948-
  Zechariah.

  Bibliography: p.
  1. Bible. O.T. Zechariah—Commentaries. I. Title.
BS1665.3.L36   1984   224′.9807   84-14750
ISBN 0-8024-0445-6 (pbk.)

3 4 5 6 7 Printing/EP/Year 92 91 90

Printed in the United States of America

CONTENTS

To the memory of my brother,

Otis C. Laney
(1956-1972)

2 Corinthians 5:1

PREFACE

Zechariah has been called an obscure book and an extremely difficult book to understand. What is its meaning? What is its message? Few Old Testament books are the subject of as many conflicting interpretations as are associated with Zechariah.

The goal of this commentary is to present a study of Zechariah's message following carefully established interpretive guidelines. This commentary may be regarded as a "cautious" approach to the book of Zechariah. The central message of each prophecy and vision will be expounded. Speculation regarding the uncertain details will be avoided.

Zechariah recorded the words and visions of a spokesman for God who ministered in Judah following the return from Babylonian captivity. The restoration period was an exciting and challenging era in Judah's history. The Temple and the city walls of Jerusalem needed rebuilding; the worship institutions needed refurbishing; and the people, still weary from long years of exile, needed encouraging. In the face of those challenges there were threats from the Arabs and syncretistic Samaritans who wanted to prevent the reestablishment of Judah. The leaders of the people faced such internal difficulties as neglect of worship, neglect of spiritual priorities, and breakdown in marriage relationships.

It was during this tempestuous period of rebuilding Jerusalem and the Jewish faith that Zechariah declared his challenging but encouraging message. He called for repentance, announced the coming of Messiah, and presented a detailed portrayal of God's future dealings with His chosen people, Israel.

INTRODUCTION

TITLE

The book receives its title from the name of the prophet who ministered to the restoration community as a contemporary of Haggai. His Hebrew name, *Zekar-Yah,* means "Yahweh remembers" and communicates a message of hope. The God of Zechariah is characterized by loyal love and will not forget His own.

AUTHOR

The name *Zechariah* was quite common among the Hebrews. It is applied to thirty different individuals in the Old Testament. Zechariah, the prophet and author of the book, is said to be "the son of Berechiah, the son of Iddo" (1:1). Ezra 5:1 and 6:14 mention him as being the son of Iddo, but no reference is made to Berechiah. Whereas some have attributed the reference to Berechiah as the result of scribal confusion between two different Zechariahs (cf. Isa. 8:2), there is abundant evidence in the Old Testament for "son" being used as an equivalent to *grandson* (cf. Gen. 31:28). Zechariah was the son of Berechiah and grandson of Iddo.

Nehemiah 12:4, 16 reveals that Iddo was among the heads of the priestly families that returned from Babylon to Judea. Thus Zechariah was a member of the tribe of Levi and probably served both as a priest and a prophet. Zechariah appears to have succeeded his grandfather Iddo as head of the priestly family (cf. Neh. 12:16), from which it may be inferred that his father, Berechiah, died at an early age.

Zechariah is generally considered to have been a young man when he received his visions of chapters 1-8 (cf. 2:4, "that young man"). He entered his prophetic ministry two months after his contemporary, Haggai, concluded his first oracles (October-November 520 B.C.).

UNITY

Critical scholars generally do not regard the book of Zechariah as a literary unit written by the one prophet named in 1:1. Whereas most scholars accept chapters 1-8 as authentic, many believe that chapters 9-14 contain anonymous prophecies from a later period that were appended to the writings of Zechariah for the purpose of preservation. It is interesting that the literary criticism of Zechariah began with the work of a scholar who was seeking to defend the accuracy of the New Testament.

Joseph Mede, a Cambridge scholar, published a dissertation in 1653 suggesting that the quotation from Zechariah 11:13 that Matthew attributes to Jeremiah (Matt. 27:9-10) indicates that chapters 9-11 were written by Jeremiah and are therefore preexilic.[1] Others advanced Mede's theory, arguing that chapters 12-14 were also a distinct literary unit written sometime before the exile. More recently scholars have abandoned the preexilic view of Mede and argue that chapters 9-14 were written long after the time of Zechariah in the Hellenistic[2] or Maccabean[3] period. Many critics would argue that two or more authors composed chapters 9-14 rather than a

1. Matthew quotes Zechariah 11:11-13 and alludes to Jeremiah 32:6-9. The gospel writer names Jeremiah as he is the major prophet and foretold what Matthew wanted to stress—the purchase of the field.
2. Otto Eissfeldt, *The Old Testament* (New York: Harper & Row, 1965), pp. 434-40.
3. Marco Treves, "Conjectures Concerning the Date and Authorship of Zechariah IX-XIV," *Vetus Testamentum,* 13 (April 1963): 196-207.

single "Deutero-Zechariah."[4] The main arguments against the unity of the book and the single authorship by Zechariah focus on three main areas: content, style, and vocabulary.

CONTENT

It is argued that whereas chapters 1-8 concern themselves with rebuilding the Temple and city of Jerusalem (1:16; 2:4; 4:6-9; 6:12), that concern is absent in chapters 9-14. The apocalyptic theme of catastrophic judgment on the Gentile nations (14:2-3, 12-14) is also considered a late development in Jewish writings. References to the good and evil shepherds in 11:4-17 have been used to argue the late date of Zechariah. The good shepherd is thought to be the high priest Onias III, who held office during the reign of Seleucus IV (187-175 B.C.). The evil shepherd of 11:17 has been identified as the high priest Menelaus (172-162 B.C.) or Alcimus (162-159 B.C.). There have been no less that thirty candidates for the three shepherds of 11:8.[5] In addition, the references to the regions conquered by Alexander the Great (9:1-2) are thought by some to indicate that chapters 9-14 were written after his conquest, much later than chapters 1-8.

STYLE

Many critical scholars have alleged that the literary style of Zechariah 9-14 is so different from chapters 1-8 that they must have been written by a different author. Whereas Zechariah 1-8 is visionary and written mostly in prose, Zechariah 9-14 is eschatological and contains a great deal of poetry. And

4. R. C. Dentan, "Introduction and Exegesis, Chapters 9-14 of Zechariah," in *The Interpreter's Bible,* ed. G. A. Buttrick, 12 vols. (Nashville: Abingdon, 1952-57), 6:1090; Yehuda T. Radday and Dieter Wickmann, "The Unity of Zechariah Examined in the Light of Statistical Linguistics," *Zeitschrift fur die alttestamentliche Wissenschaft,* 87 (1975): 30-55.

5. R. K. Harrison, *Introduction to the Old Testament* (Grand Rapids: Eerdmans, 1969), p. 953.

in contrast to the earlier chapters, there is no interpreting angel in chapters 9-14. Nor is there any reference made to Zechariah himself, whereas in chapters 1-8 he is named three times (1:1, 7; 7:1) and is an active participant in the visions.[6]

VOCABULARY

The vocabulary of Zechariah has also been used to argue against its unity. It has been pointed out that whereas the phrase "thus says the LORD [Yahweh]" occurs frequently in chapters 1-8, it is found only once in chapters 9-14 (11:4). It has also been noted that the words "in that day" occur at least eighteen times in Zechariah 9-14, whereas they are found only three times in Zechariah 1-8. The mention of "Greece" in Zechariah 9:13 as the dominant power rather than Persia is thought to indicate a late date for chapters 9-14.

A Response:

The arguments of the critical scholars against the unity of Zechariah may not be as ominous as they might at first appear. J. Stafford Wright offers this word of caution: "It is not possible to prove the unity of the book, but one should not too readily abandon it."[7] Several noted scholars, including R. K. Harrison, Gleason Archer, and E. J. Young have written well-reasoned defenses of the unity and single authorship of Zechariah. Their arguments are worthy of consideration.

With regard to content, it should be noted that variations in purpose may result in variation in content. Chapters 1-8 are historically oriented, designed to encourage the returned exiles to turn from their sinful ways of the past and enjoy cleansing and blessing. Chapters 9-14 are eschatologically oriented, designed to encourage the despairing remnant con-

6. Joyce Baldwin, *Haggai, Zechariah, Malachi* (London: InterVarsity, 1972), p. 63.
7. J. Stafford Wright, "The Book of Zechariah," in *The Illustrated Bible Dictionary,* ed. N. Hillyer, 3 vols. (Wheaton: Tyndale, 1980), 3:1679.

cerning the future glories of Zion. Thus, some difference in content between chapters 1-8 and 9-14 is not an overwhelming argument against the unity of the book. Arguments for late dating Zechariah 9-14 are seriously undermined by the inability of the critics to agree on the historical identifications of the shepherds of chapter 11. Their identifications are conjectural and speculative. And while Zechariah 9:1-2 may appear to refer to the provinces conquered by Alexander, only a rationalistic denial of predictive prophecy would require that that passage be written *after* rather than before the event.

As to alleged differences in style, one would be rather naive to think that an author's style would remain static over a period of years. Certainly an ability to vary one's style depending on the content and mood is one mark of a gifted writer. Whereas differences in style are frequently noted in Zechariah, similarities are often overlooked. Young observes that there is a peculiar five-member type parallelism that is scarcely found outside Zechariah but that occurs once in chapters 1-8 and three times in Zechariah 9-14 (cf. 6:13; 9:5, 7; 12:4).[8] In addition, the Hebrew verb *yashab* ("to sit," "to dwell") is used in the special sense of "be inhabited" twice in chapters 1-8 and twice in chapters 9-14. Seldom does the verb have this meaning outside Zechariah.[9] The promise in 8:8, "They will be My people and I will be their God," is repeated in 13:9. Thus it appears that the similarities in style between the two sections of Zechariah are as great or greater than their differences.

Finally, with regard to vocabulary, it should be observed that while the phrase "thus says the LORD [Yahweh]," occurs frequently in chapters 1-8 and only once in chapters 9-14, the phrase "says the LORD [Yahweh]," occurs fourteen times in the first section and six times in the second section. "Yahweh of Hosts" appears three times in each section of the book.

8. Edward J. Young, *An Introduction to the Old Testament* (Grand Rapids: Eerdmans, 1949), p. 273.
9. Gleason L. Archer, Jr., *A Survey of Old Testament Introduction,* rev. ed. (Chicago: Moody, 1974), p. 430.

Harrison notes that the use of "two" as a favorite number in both portions of the work (4:3; 5:9; 6:1, 11:7; 13:8), the persistent use of the vocative form of address (2:7, 10; 3:2, 8; 4:7; 9:9, 13; 11:1; 13:7), and the presence of the phrase "went back and forth" (7:14; 9:8), which occurs nowhere else in the Hebrew Scriptures, are evidences of the literature unity of the book.[10]

It is rather significant that in spite of the arguments against the unity of Zechariah, "all fourteen chapters have been handed down to us as one book in every manuscript so far discovered."[11] Although the Hebrew manuscript discovered at Qumran includes only a fragment of Zechariah (1:1-4), the Greek manuscript found there includes the end of chapter 8 and the beginning of chapter 9 with no gap or spacing whatsoever to suggest a break between the two parts. The evidence suggests that the interpreter would do well to treat Zechariah as a unified composition written by a single author whose name appears in the book as Zechariah (1:1; 7:1).

DATE OF WRITING

Determining the date of Zechariah is a problem intrinsically united with the matter of the unity of the book. Those who deny the unity of Zechariah argue that chapters 9-14 date from the Hellenistic or Maccabean period. Eissfeldt prefers 332 B.C. because of the allusions to Alexander the Great's siege of Tyre in 9:3.[12] Marco Treves argues that chapters 9-14 were written, at least in part, by Judas Maccabeus and dates it around 166-164 B.C.[13]

A major argument of those who late date the book is based on the reference to Greece ("Javan") in 9:13. It is held that the reference to Greece as the dominant power rather than Persia suggests a date after Alexander's conquest (c. 330

10. Harrison, *Introduction to the Old Testament,* p. 954.
11. Baldwin, *Haggai, Zechariah, Malachi,* pp. 69-70.
12. Eissfeldt, *The Old Testament,* p. 437.
13. Treves, "Conjectures Concerning the Date and Authorship of Zechariah IX-XIV," pp. 205-7.

B.C.). It has been pointed out, however, that Greek influence was felt in the Near East as early as the seventh century B.C. Greece ("Javan") was named by both Isaiah (66:19) and Ezekiel (27:13, 19). Harrison notes that Greek mercenary troops constituted the bulk of the Persian armed forces, and thus could have been seen by Zechariah as a coming menace to the Persian regime.[14] Sporadic raids by the Greeks on the Palestinian coastland began about 500 B.C.with the great Ionian revolt. Certainly the defeat of Xerxes by the Greeks at the battle of Salamis in 480 B.C. would serve to bring them to the attention of all the inhabitants of the Persian Empire.

Those who hold to the unity of the book date Zechariah between 520 and 470 B.C. The biblical text states that Zechariah commenced his prophetic ministry in the second year of Darius (522-486 B.C.) or 520 B.C. (1:1). His last dated prophecy (7:1) was two years later in 518 B.C. The latter chapters of the prophecy (9-14) may have been composed sometime later. Archer suggests a date between 480 and 470 for chapters 9-14.[15]

S. Bullough correctly maintains that the visions of chapters 1-8 were composed between 520 and 518 B.C. when Zechariah was about thirty years of age. He suggests that the prophecies of chapters 9-14 were written when he was about seventy, when the future of the Persian Empire had become less secure. That would place them after the revolt of Egypt in 486 B.C., the death of Darius in 485 B.C., and the failure of Xerxes' expedition against Greece in 480 B.C.[16] The difference in the author's age and the changing political circumstances are sufficient to account for any differences between chapters 1-8 and 9-14. It is most probable that the book of Zechariah was composed during the prophet's lifetime (between 520 and 470 B.C.).

14. Harrison, *Introduction to the Old Testament,* p. 953.
15. Archer, *A Survey of Old Testament Introduction,* p. 429.
16. S. Bullough, "Zechariahs," in *A Catholic Commentary on Holy Scripture,* ed. Bernard Orchard (New York: Thomas Nelson, 1953), p. 691.

HISTORICAL SETTING

Zechariah lived and ministered during the restoration period that followed the Babylonian Exile. As the prophets had predicted exile because of disobedience, so they predicted the return to the land after seventy years of discipline (Isa. 43:14-21; Jer. 25:11-12; 29:10). God began to fulfill that promise of restoration when He raised up Cyrus, king of Anshan, who conquered Achmetha and inherited the kingdom of the Medes in 550 B.C. (cf. Isa. 41:2; 44:28; 45:1-7). Cyrus went on to defeat Croesus, king of Lydia, and captured his capital at Sardis in 546 B.C. In 539 B.C. Cyrus captured Babylon and founded the Persian Empire. Cyrus's victory was divinely determined by God for the purpose of effecting the return of the Jews from captivity.

Anxious to win over the subjects of his vast new kingdom, Cyrus allowed the practice of religions that had been suppressed by the Babylonians. He reestablished sanctuaries for many neglected gods and returned captured idols to their respective temples. In his own words Cyrus declared: "I settled upon the command of Marduk, the great lord, all the gods of Sumer and Akkad whom Nabonidus has brought into Babylon to the anger of the lord of the gods, unharmed, in their [former] chapels, the places which make them happy."[17]

In addition to returning gods to their temples, Cyrus returned exiled peoples to their lands. "I [also] gathered all their [former] inhabitants and returned [to them] their habitations."[18] Included among those who benefited from the generous policy of Cyrus were the Judeans. In 538 B.C., his first official year after his ascension year in 539, Cyrus decreed the return of the Jewish exiles to Judah (Ezra 1:1-4; 2 Chron. 36:22-23). In 537 B.C. the first group of Jews returned to Jerusalem under the leadership of Sheshbazzar, the prince of Judah (Ezra 1:8). (For discussion on the relation-

---

17. James B. Pritchard, ed., *Ancient Near Eastern Texts,* 3d edition with supplement (Princeton, N.J.: Princeton U., 1969), p. 316.
18. Ibid.

ship of Zerubbabel, also referred to as "governor of Judah" (Hag. 1:4), see the comments on Zechariah 4:9.) The altar was erected in the fall of 537 B.C. in preparation for the feasts of Trumpets and Tabernacles, but reconstruction of the Temple itself did not begin until the spring of the next year, 536 B.C. (Ezra 3:1, 6-8).

The returned exiles were soon to learn that no work of God goes unopposed. Shortly after the foundation of the Temple had been laid, the syncretistic Samaritans to the north asked if they could join in the project. Zerubbabel and Jeshua the high priest wisely refused to allow those who "feared the LORD [Yahweh] and served their own gods" (2 Kings 17:33) to become involved in the work. Those "enemies of Judah and Benjamin" then discouraged the people, frightened the builders, and hired counselors against them to frustrate their work (Ezra 4:4-5). This opposition resulted in the Jews abandoning work on the Temple until 520 B.C., the second year of Darius (Ezra 4:24). For sixteen years the Temple building lay neglected as the returned exiles rebuilt and remodeled their homes. During that period the people of Judah lost their vision and sense of spiritual purpose. They procrastinated saying, "The time has not come, even the time for the house of the LORD [Yahweh] to be rebuilt" (Hag. 1:2). The result of such neglect was divine chastening. God "called for a drought" and sent upon the land "blasting wind, mildew, and hail" (Hag. 1:11; 2:17). The crops failed, the people languished, and yet they did not repent (Hag. 2:17).

In 520 B.C. God raised up two prophetic spokesmen to turn His people back to Himself. Haggai called for the people to recognize their spiritual priorities and to rebuild the Temple. He declared, "Is it time for you yourselves to dwell in your paneled houses while this house lies desolate?" (Hag. 1:4). He urged the people to reflect on their distressful circumstances and recognize them as divine chastening (Hag. 1:5, 7). Haggai's contemporary Zechariah began his prophetic ministry just two months after his colleague's first message (Hag. 1:1; Zech. 1:1) and was used by God to call the people to sincere repentance. He warned, "Return now from your evil ways and from your evil deeds" (Zech. 1:4). It was through the prophetic ministry of those two men that the leaders and people of Judah repented from their misdeeds and neglect of priorities. They "arose and began to rebuild the house of God which is in Jerusalem" (Ezra 5:2; cf. Hag. 1:14).

The ministries of the two prophets did not cease when the construction began. In reporting the events of that great day, Ezra the scribe commented: "And the prophets of God were with them supporting them" (Ezra 5:2). Haggai and Zechariah continued in a supportive role, encouraging the people with prophetic messages. Haggai's recorded messages were delivered in 520 B.C. Zechariah's last dated prophecy was given in 518 B.C. (Zech. 7:1). On the basis of their sincere repentance, God began again to pour out His blessing on His people (Hag. 2:19). The Temple was completed in 515 B.C. and rededicated to God's worship with great rejoicing (Ezra 8:16-18).

As Zechariah began his ministry, Darius, the Persian ruler (522-486 B.C.), had a firm control over his empire, which included Persia, Mesopotamia, Palestine, Egypt, and Asia Minor. It could well be said during his early reign, "All the earth is peaceful and quiet" (Zech. 1:11). The conditions in Judah at that time, however, were disheartening. The Temple was still unbuilt (Hag. 1:4), and the city walls of Jerusalem were in ruins (Neh. 2:17). The people of Judah were experiencing drought and adversity (Hag. 1:6, 11) instead of divine blessing. It was to such a despairing people that Zechariah offered a message of messianic hope and promise.

LITERARY FORMS

It would be difficult to describe Zechariah in terms of just one literary genre. There are several different literary forms that are observed in the book. The introductory call to repentance (1:1-6) is followed by a series of eight dream-visions recorded by the prophet (1:7-6:8). The most notable feature of those visions is the use of an interpreting angel to explain the meaning of the vision to Zechariah (1:9, 13, 14; 2:3; 4:1, 5; 5:5, 10; 6:4). Some scholars have referred to this material as *apocalyptic,* a term derived from the Greek word *apokalypsis* (Rev. 1:1), which means "uncovering," or "revelation." According to Ralph Alexander, apocalyptic literature is "symbolic, visionary, prophetic literature, composed during oppressive conditions consisting of visions whose events are recorded exactly as they were seen by the author and explained through a divine interpreter, and whose theological content is primarily eschatological."[19] As so defined, apocalyptic literature in Scripture includes Ezekiel 37:1-14, 40-48; Daniel 2:7-8, 10-12; Zechariah 1:7-6:8; and the book of Revelation. Alexander suggests that this literary form arose out of the Mesopotamian dream-visions that frequently appear in ancient Near Eastern literature dating from 7-6 centuries B.C.[20] God is the communicator par excellence and may well have employed this culturally understood literary form to reveal His truth to His people in a creative and contemporary manner.[21]

Apocalyptic or dream-vision materials customarily include three major elements: (1) the description of the setting; (2) the record of the vision; and (3) the interpretation of the vision. Those elements are clearly seen in the first chapter of Revelation:

I. The Description of the Setting (Rev. 1:1-11)
  A. Date of the vision—"the Lord's day" (1:10)
  B. Recipient of the vision—"John" (1:1, 9)
  C. Place of the vision—"Patmos" (1:9)

---

19. Ralph H. Alexander, "Hermeneutics of Old Testament Apocalyptic Literature," Th.D. dissertation, Dallas Theological Seminary, 1968, p. 45.
20. Ibid, pp. 134-52.
21. For other examples see J. Carl Laney, *First and Second Samuel* (Chicago: Moody, 1982), pp. 10-12, and "The Role of the Prophets in God's Case Against Israel," *Bibliotheca Sacra* 138 (October-December 1981): 313-25.

D. Noteworthy circumstances (1:1-11)
II. The Record of the Vision—"I saw" (Rev. 1:12-17)
III. The Interpretation of the Vision (Rev. 1:18-20)

This pattern is found in Zechariah 1:7-17 and is generally followed in the rest of Zechariah's night visions (1:7—6:8).

Students of Scripture ought to exercise caution to avoid free-wheeling speculation in interpreting apocalyptic literature. Certainly a normal, grammatico-historical interpretation should be followed. In addition, Alexander advises that the expositor not *add* to the interpretation provided by the divine interpreter—the interpreting angel (1:9, 13, 14; 2:3; 4:1, 5; 5:5, 10; 6:4).[22] As a further precaution against speculative excesses, he suggests that the expositor not seek to interpret the minute details of the visions.[23] The fact that the rider in the first vision is on a "red" horse and that the trees were "myrtle" does not appear to have any significance other than contributing to the reality and vividness of the vision. The only exception to this latter interpretive guideline might be when one is confronted with a symbol that has revelatory significance on the basis of antecedent theology or analogy of Scripture.

Another literary form found in Zechariah is symbolic action. Ezekiel abounds with such symbolic actions (Ezek. 4:1-3, 4-8, 9-17; 5:1-17; 12:1-7, 17-20). Isaiah and Micah went "naked and barefoot" as a symbolic gesture of humiliation and mourning due to coming judgment (Isa. 20:2-4; Mic. 1:8). Hosea's marriage was symbolic of the unfaithfulness of Israel and the unceasing love of Yahweh (Hos. 1-3). Similarly, the crowning of Joshua the high priest had instructive purposes (Zech. 6:9-15). It was a symbolic action connected with the thought and theme of the preceding visions.

Many have considered chapters 7-8 to be a sermon on fast-

22. Alexander, "Hermeneutics of Old Testament Apocalyptic Literature," p. 265.
23. Ibid., pp. 161-62, 196-98, 265.

ing. However, this section may be more accurately viewed as an inquiry made to the priests followed by the prophet's words on the need for sincere worship and true righteousness over against superficial acts of devotion and piety. A similar inquiry—exhortation pattern is found in the prophecy of Haggai (Hag. 2:12-14).

The last section of Zechariah, chapters 9-14, contain two prophetic "burdens" (9-11; 12-14). Each of those sections is introduced by the phrase "the burden of the word of the LORD [Yahweh]" (9:1; 12:1). The term *burden* is derived from the Hebrew word that means "to lift up," "to bear a burden." Whereas some have suggested that the word is better translated "oracle" (hence, "an oracle: the word of Yahweh"), it has been demonstrated that there is little evidence for such a view. In his study of more than sixty occurrences of the word in the Old Testament, P. A. H. de Boer discovered that *massa'* is a burden "imposed by a master, a despot or a deity on their subjects, beasts, men or things."[24] In prophecy *massa'* acquires an ominous sense as it is linked with catastrophic judgment. It is a prophetic burden imposed on the prophet that he must discharge with a measure of compulsion, urgency, and dread. In chapters 9-14 Zechariah sets forth the weighty judgments on Israel and the nations that must precede the coming of Messiah and His kingdom.

PURPOSE

The purpose of Zechariah is twofold. First, the prophecy is intended to exhort the returned exiles to turn from their sins to the Lord for cleansing and blessing. Through the prophet, Yahweh declares, "Return to Me . . . that I may return to you" (1:3). Second, the prophecy is designed to comfort and encourage the returned remnant regarding the rebuilding of

---

24. P. A. H. de Boer, *An Inquiry into the Meaning of the Term Massa'* (Leiden: Brill, 1948), p. 214. See also *Theological Wordbook of the Old Testament,* ed. R. L. Harris, Gleason L. Archer, and Bruce K. Waltke, s.v. *massa',* by W. C. Kaiser, 2:602.

the Temple and God's future work among His people in Jerusalem (1:16-17; 2:12; 3:2; 4:9; 6:14-15). The visions and
prophecies contain "comforting words" (1:13) revealing the
future glories of Zion, the ultimate overthrow of Israel's
enemies, and the universal reign of Messiah. The prophecy of
Zechariah presents a detailed portrayal of God's future dealings with His chosen people, Israel.

THEME

The key thought in the first chapters of the book is God's
choice of Jerusalem (1:17; 2:12; 3:2). Like Romans 11,
Zechariah reveals that God has not set His people aside because of their disobedience. God will not only reaffirm
Jerusalem's election but promises to come among His repentant people and dwell in their midst. "I will return to Zion
and dwell in the midst of Jerusalem" (8:3; cf. 2:10-11; 8:23).
Messiah "the Branch" (6:12) is seen to be the One who will
accomplish God's spiritual work among His people. The
theme of Zechariah could be summarized as "the restoration
of God's people Israel through the redeeming and delivering
work of Messiah."

THEOLOGY

Zechariah is a very theological book. It is rich in truth both
about God's Person and His plan for the ages. But it is truth
that focuses on practical issues rather than theoretical dogma.
The prophet Zechariah appears to have written with a view to
practical application of the message he communicates. The
major theological thrusts include Christology, soteriology,
true religion, and eschatology.

CHRISTOLOGY

Zechariah taught a great deal concerning the first and sec-
ond advents of the Messiah. He referred to Messiah as the
"Branch" (3:8), God's "Servant" (v. 8), and God's
"Shepherd" (13:7). He also alluded to Christ's ministry as a

King-Priest (6:13; cf. Heb. 6:20—7:1). The significance of Zechariah in the life and ministry of Christ is evidenced by the fact that chapters 9-14 are the most quoted section of the Prophets in the Passion narratives of the gospels.[25] Concerning Christ's first advent, Zechariah prophesied His entrance into Jerusalem on a colt (9:9; cf. Matt. 21:4-5; John 12:14-16), His betrayal for thirty pieces of silver (11:12-13; cf. Matt. 27:9), the piercing of His hands and feet (12:10; cf. John 19:37), and the cleansing from sin provided by His death on the cross (13:1; cf. John 1:29, Titus 3:5).

Concerning Messiah's second advent, Zechariah prophesied the conversion of Israel at His return (12:10-13:1, 9; cf. Rom. 11:26), the destruction of Israel's enemies by Messiah (14:3, 12-15; cf. Rev. 19:11-16), and the kingdom reign of Christ from Jerusalem (14:9, 16; cf. Rev. 20:4-6).

SOTERIOLOGY

Zechariah is a book with a message about God's plan of salvation. The prerequisite of repentance is emphasized in the introduction. " 'Return to Me,' declares Yahweh of hosts, 'that I may return to you' " (1:3). Failure to turn from evil to God (i.e., "repent"; cf. 1 Thess. 1:9) is seen to result in certain judgment (1:4-6). The doctrine of election is prominent in the early chapters of Zechariah (1:17; 2:12; 3:2). God's choice of Jerusalem emphasizes His sovereignty over His people. God's elective purposes are grounded in His absolute sovereignty, are consistent with His perfect justice, and are motivated by His unconditional love (cf. Rom. 9:10-25; Eph. 1:4-5, 11).

Zechariah 3:1-5 contains one of the most instructive passages in the Old Testament concerning the removal of sin and imputation of righteousness. Joshua the high priest is seen as clothed in filthy garments and standing before the Angel of Yahweh. The text reveals that the garments repre-

25. Baldwin, *Haggai, Zechariah, Malachi,* p. 59.

sent the pollution of sin (3:4). The angel of Yahweh commands the removal of the filthy garments and that Joshua be
clothed with clean festal robes. That is done without Joshua's
assistance and is seen as an act of divine grace (see also 12:10).
The iniquity of sin is removed, and positive righteousness,
represented by the clean garments, is imparted to Joshua.
That scene vividly illustrates the work of Christ in taking on
man's sin and placing on the believer's account (i.e., "im-
puting") His own positive righteousness (cf. Rom. 5:18-19;
2 Cor. 5:21).

TRUE RELIGION

The prophets of Israel had an eye for the practical application of their faith, and Zechariah was no exception. For
Zechariah true religion was not bound up with external acts
of religious piety, but with genuine concern for others based
on one's personal relationship with the great and awesome
God. Yahweh questioned the motives of the people's fasting
and mourning in commemoration of the sorrowful events of
586 B.C.: "When you fasted and mourned in the fifth and
seventh months these seventy years, was it actually for Me
that you fasted?" (7:5). The obvious answer to that rhetorical
question is, "No!" Their acts of piety were centered on themselves rather than God.

God's desire for His people is that they "dispense true
justice, and practice kindness and compassion each to his
brother," and that they "speak the truth to one another"
(7:9; 8:16). Zechariah condemned the oppression of the
widow, the orphan, the stranger, or the poor, and the devising of evil against one another (7:10). Like the other prophets
of Israel, Zechariah was a preacher of righteousness. He was
convinced that true religion was a way of living and relating
to God and mankind. Superficial acts of piety or religious
ritual have no place in true religion.

ESCHATOLOGY

Zechariah is a book that focuses the reader's attention on

the doctrine of last things. It appears that next to Ezekiel, Zechariah has influenced the author of Revelation more than any other Old Testament book. Of the approximately seventy-one quotations of Zechariah in the New Testament, thirty-one are found in Revelation (twenty from chapters 1-8; eight from chapters 9-14).[26]

Zechariah's eschatological focus can best be appreciated through an understanding of a concept that has long been recognized as a major theme of Old Testament prophetic thought—the "Day of Yahweh" or the "Day of the Lord." Although Zechariah does not use the precise words "Day of Yahweh," he uses a slight variation in 14:1 ("day to Yahweh") and refers frequently to "that day" (2:11; 3:10; 9:16; 12:3, 6, 8, 9, 11; 13:1, 2, 4; 14:4, 6, 8-9, 13, 20-21), an expression clearly related to the Day of the Lord tradition. Recent studies on the Day of the Lord have focused on the origin of the concept in the Prophets. There are four major suggestions: (1) holy war tradition, (2) an enthronement festival for Yahweh, (3) the execution of the covenant curses, and (4) the motif of theophany descriptions.[27] It seems most probable that the concept of the Day of the Lord originated with the conquest of Canaan—a conquest that was, in fact, Yahweh's war (Deut. 1:30; 3:22; Josh. 5:13-15; 6:2; cf. Ex. 14:14; 15:3).

Although most of the eighteen specific references to "the Day of the Lord" speak of future historical or eschatological events, five texts describe and interpret the Day of the Lord in terms of past historical events (Isa. 22:1-14; Jer. 46:2-12; Lam. 1-2; Ezek. 13:1-9). Those texts reflect circumstances of military tragedy, defeat, and judgment. Such events may have provided the basis for the prophetic concept of a future historical or even eschatological "day" of divine judgment on the disobedience of Israel and the nations (Isa. 13:6, 9; Joel

26. W. S. LaSor, D. A. Hubbard, and F. William Bush, *Old Testament Survey* (Grand Rapids: Eerdmans, 1982), p. 499.
27. A Joseph Everson, "The Days of Yahweh," *Journal of Biblical Literature* 93 (1974): 329-37.

1:15; Zeph. 1:14-18). But the Day of the Lord is not just a day of wrath and judgment on the disobedient. In eschatological contexts it is also seen to include deliverance and restoration for the righteous. The Day of the Lord is a day of future hope, prosperity, and blessing (Isa. 4:2-6; Hos. 2:18-23; Joel 3:18-21; Amos 9:11-15; Mic. 4:6-8).

The eschatological Day of the Lord may be defined as that period of time during which God will deal with Israel and the nations through judgment and deliverance. Whereas the second advent is preceded by signs (Matt. 24:29-30), the Day of the Lord is said to come unexpectedly (1 Thess. 5:2). Thus, it must begin shortly after the rapture of the church, an imminent and signless event. According to the apostle Peter, the Day of the Lord will conclude with the purging of the heavens and earth in preparation for the creation of the new heavens and earth (2 Pet. 3:10-13). Thus, the eschatological Day of the Lord includes the prophesied events of the Tribulation period, the events of the second advent, the millennial kingdom, the final revolt of Satan, the great white throne judgment, and the purging of the earth in preparation for the new creation (cf. Rev. 6-20). It is both a day of destruction and salvation, a day of wrath and grace. It would be well for us to distinguish the eschatological Day of the Lord from "the day of Christ" (Phil. 2:16; cf. 1:6), which relates to the rapture of the church, and "the day of God" (2 Pet. 3:12), which relates to God's rule over the new heavens and earth throughout eternity.

Concerning the nation of Israel in the Day of the Lord, Zechariah reveals that God's chosen people will experience a period of judgment (the Tribulation) followed by the deliverance of a remnant (12:1-9; 13:8-9). A remnant of Israel will repent and be converted at the second advent (12:10—13:1) and be brought back to the Promised Land (10:8-10) to enjoy the blessings of Messiah's future kingdom (14:6-11).

Concerning the Gentile nations, Zechariah predicts future divine judgment on all the nations that have opposed God's people (12:9; cf. 2:8-9). But Zechariah also predicts that many Gentiles will someday worship God in Messiah's kingdom (2:11; 8:22-23; 14:16) and be subject to Messiah's rule (14:17-19). It is clear from both Genesis 12:1-3 and the message of Zechariah that the blessings that God has for Israel extend through Christ to believing Gentiles (cf. Gal. 3:7-9).

Zechariah reveals a great deal concerning the future kingdom reign of "the Branch" (Messiah). This kingdom is described in Revelation 20:4 as lasting a thousand years, hence the *millennial* kingdom. The thousand years is the first installment of what will be an eternal kingdom (2 Sam. 7:16; Isa. 9:7; Luke 1:32-33; 2 Pet. 1:11; cf. 1 Cor. 15:24-28). After regathering the remnant of Israel to the Promised Land (10:10-12), the Messiah will reign as King over all the earth from Jerusalem (8:3; 14:9). All the nations will come to worship Him there (8:20-23; 14:16). During the kingdom reign of Messiah the "curse" on the earth will be lifted (cf. Gen. 3:17-19), and the land will enjoy renewed productivity and prosperity (14:11; 9:17—10:1). The Messiah will rule His kingdom with a firm hand, punishing any expression of unrighteousness or rebellion (14:17-19). The kingdom of Messiah will be characterized by holiness and total dedication to the Lord (14:20-21).

STRUCTURE

The overall structure of Zechariah is fairly clear. The introduction (1:1-6) is followed by three major sections: Zechariah's night visions (1:7—6:15), the inquiry-exhortation on fasting (7:1—8:23), and the eschatological prophecies regarding Israel and the nations (9-14). Each of those major units of Zechariah may be divided into subsections based on key words and phrases. Each of the seven night visions begins with words descriptive of "seeing." Zechariah declares, "I saw" (1:8); "I lifted up my eyes and looked" (1:18; 2:1; 5:1; 6:1); "then he showed me" (3:1); "I see" (4:2). The inquiry-exhortation on fasting may be divided into four sections based on the key phrase (with slight variations) "Then the

word of the LORD came saying" (7:1, 8; 8:1, 18). Finally, the
eschatological prophecies can be divided into two main sections based on the key phrase "the burden of the word of the
LORD" (9:1; 12:1).

It is significant, in view of the arguments against the unity
of Zechariah, that P. Lamarche has presented evidence for
the unity of Zechariah 9-14 based on an observable pattern of
chiasmus.[28] The concept of chiasmus is derived from the
Greek letter *chi,* which corresponds to the English *X.*
Chiasmus involves a crossing-over or inverted correspondence of thoughts (i.e., A:B:B:A). This is evidenced in Isaiah
50:1 where the Lord declares to Israel:

> A. Where is the certificate of divorce
>   by which I sent your mother away?
> B. Or to whom of My creditors did I sell you?
> B. Behold, you were sold for your iniquities,
>
> A. And for your transgressions your mother was sent
>   away.

Another good example of chiasmus is found in Isaiah 55:8-9.
E. W. Bullinger presents a thorough discussion on chiasmus
and provides many illustrations from both the Old and New
Testaments.[29]

According to Lamarche, Zechariah made use of chiasmus
in the prophetic burdens of chapters 9-14. The introductory
statement of judgment and salvation in 9:1-8 is seen to
balance with the conclusion in 14:16-21. The material between is seen to consist of two sections: 9:9—11:17 and
12:1—14:15. As analyzed and explained by Joyce Baldwin,[30]

28. P. Lamarche, *Zacharie IX-XIV. Structure Literaire at Messianisme*
    (Paris: Gabalda, 1961), pp. 112-13.
29. E. W. Bullinger, *Figures of Speech in the Bible* (Grand Rapids: Baker,
    1968), pp. 374-79.
30. Baldwin, *Haggai, Zechariah, Malachi,* pp. 77-81.

each section contains similar themes: (1) the king, shepherd, and Lord's representative, all of whom are identified as one and the same person (9:9-10; 11:14-17; 12:10-13:1; 13:7-9; (2) Israel's war and victory (9:11-10:1; 10:3*b*-11:3; 12:1-9; 14:1-15); (3) judgment on idols (10:2, 3*a*; 13:2-6). These themes are developed in chapters 9-11 and intensified in chapters 9-14.

The chiastic pattern evidenced in chapters 9-14 may also be presented in chapters 1-6 as suggested by Bullinger[31]:

A. Peace in the Gentile kingdoms (1:7-17)
  B. Judgment on Gentile nations (1:18-21)
    C. Remnant delivered from Babylon (2:1-13)
      D. Priesthood and royalty remodeled (3:1-10)
      D. Priesthood and royalty remodeled (4:1-14)
    C. Wickedness removed to Babylon (5:5-11)
  B. Judgment on Gentile nations (6:1-8)
A. Peace of Messiah's kingdom (6:9-15)

The pattern of chiasmus is not perfect, for 5:1-4 does not seem to fit, but the evidence for such inverted correspondence at several points is simply too strong to ignore. Baldwin concludes, "The chiastic pattern, though most prominent in the second part of the book, is present in the whole."[32] An understanding of the chiastic structure of Zechariah will not only enhance the reader's appreciation of the author's literary artistry but may serve as an arsenal of evidence for the unity of the book and provide the interpreter with insights based on the analysis of parallel thoughts.

OUTLINE

I. The Introductory Call to Repentance (1:1-6)
  A. The Superscription (1:1)

31. Bullinger, *Figures of Speech,* p. 376.
32. Baldwin, *Haggai, Zechariah, Malachi,* p. 81.

1

THE INTRODUCTORY CALL
TO REPENTANCE

(Zechariah 1:1-6)

The return to their Judean homeland in 537 B.C. constituted a new beginning for the Jewish exiles. As the Exodus from Egypt had resulted in the establishment of the Israelite nation, so this "second exodus" (cf. Isa. 11:16; 51:9-11) resulted in the refounding of Judah. But the returned exiles faltered as they made this fresh start. Although the foundation of the Temple had been laid, a neglect of spiritual priorities prevented its completion (Hag. 1:4). The lax spiritual condition of the Judeans could never be blessed by the Lord. Zechariah knew that genuine repentance was the prerequisite for spiritual blessing.

Zechariah's words were hard but necessary ones for a people who had failed to take God seriously. Verse 3 is the key to this section. God promised a change in His manner of dealing with His people if they would but change their ways.

The Superscription (1:1)

Zechariah began his prophetic ministry in 520 B.C., or in the eighth month of the second year of Darius (522-486 B.C.). The eighth month, known on ancient Jewish calendars as Marchesvan, coincides with October-November on our Julian calendar. The eighth month began on October 27, 520 B.C. Unlike the other dates given in Haggai and Zechariah, the day of the month is not given here. The absence of a date has led some to suggest that it was the new moon—the first day of the month. Although this view has the support of the Syriac version, it is better to set a pattern early in this study of avoiding speculation in commenting on Zechariah.

Zechariah identifies himself as a prophet who brings the authoritative "word of the LORD" to the people. Although the derivation of the Hebrew word for prophet (*nabi*) is debated, the meaning is quite clear from Scripture. A prophet is one who speaks forth the message that God has revealed to him (cf. Ex. 7:1-2).[1] As a spokesman for God, Zechariah's primary duty was to faithfully declare God's message to God's people.

Zechariah the prophet appears to have a significant spiritual heritage. As the grandson of Iddo, one of the heads of the priestly families that returned from Babylon to Judea (Neh. 12:4, 16), Zechariah was a member of the tribe of Levi and probably served both as a priest and a prophet. His priestly lineage may have given him a special burden for the rebuilding of the temple in Jerusalem and the full restoration of worship.

THE PROPHET'S CALL (1:2-3)

In dealing with His sinful people, God does not mince words or sidestep issues. The first prophetic utterance is a strong affirmation of Yahweh's anger against the "fathers." In this context, the "fathers" refers not to the patriarchs, but to the forefathers of the generation to whom Zechariah ministered (cf. 7:9-12; 8:14). This was the generation that heard but did not heed the rebukes of the prophets and fell under judgment (cf. 2 Chron. 36:15-16). Jerusalem was destroyed, and the Judeans were taken into exile.

The verb "was angry" is supplemented in the Hebrew text by a noun made up of the same three letters, which strengthens the verb's force. The phrase could be translated, "Yahweh was extremely angry with your fathers."

1. J. Carl Laney, "The Role of the Prophets in God's Case Against Israel," *Bibliotheca Sacra* 138 (October-December 1981): 314.

The anger of God is a subject that is frequently overlooked and neglected by Christians today. God's attribute of love is often pitted against this attribute, thus diminishing its importance. How can a loving God execute wrathful judgment? The key is to recognize that God's wrath against sin is in keeping with His infinitely holy character. He cannot look on sin with indifference. That which falls short of the standard of God's own character must be judged. Yet Scripture reveals that God does not judge hastily. He is "slow to anger" (Nah. 1:3). The fact that this earth continues to exist in spite of man's sin and rebellion is a testimony to God's infinite grace. As the apostle Peter declares, "The Lord is not slow about His promise, as some count slowness, but is patient toward you, not wishing for any to perish but for all to come to repentance" (2 Pet. 3:9). God's wrath and God's love are affirmed in both testaments (Ex. 34:6; Deut. 7:7-11; John 3:16, 36). Neither of those attributes can be denied without diminishing the true character of God.

The theme of Zechariah's first prophetic message reflects the central thrust of his ministry. It is found in verse 3 where Yahweh issues a call to repentance. The imperative "return" implies a change of mind that issues in a change of conduct. Such repentance is illustrated by the Thessalonians who "turned to God from idols to serve a living and true God" (1 Thess. 1:9). The words "to Me" personalize the call to repentance. God desires a personal relationship with His people. But repentance from sin is the prerequisite for such fellowship. A sincere return to the Lord will result in a relationship in which the repentant sinner can experience God's blessing (cf. Hag. 2:17-19). The theme in verse 3 must have had a significant impact on the people for it appeared years later in the preaching of Malachi (Mal. 3:7).

God is designated "LORD [Yahweh] of hosts" three times in verse 3. This is a military designation referring to God as the One who commands the angelic armies of heaven (1 Kings 22:19; Luke 2:13; Rev. 19:14) and the armies of Israel (Judg. 5:14; 1 Sam. 17:45). Whereas the "LORD of hosts" designation appears 261 times in the Old Testament, the greatest concentration of occurrences is in the postexilic prophets: Haggai (14), Zechariah (53), and Malachi (24). The expression emphasizes the sovereignty and omnipotence of God as the supreme commander of every earthly, heavenly, or cosmic force. J. E. Hartley observes, "Although the title has military overtones, it points directly to Yahweh's rulership over the entire universe."[2] It is a most exalted title. Zechariah seems to be saying to the people, "Return to the God from whom you have departed. The King of the Universe desires fellowship with *you*!"

THE PROPHET'S WARNING (1:4-6)

In verses 4-6 Zechariah warns the postexilic community against following the example of their forefathers who refused to repent and were taken into exile. "Do not be like your fathers," exhorts Zechariah. The "former prophets" would be those spokesmen of God who ministered during the closing years of the Judean monarchy, such as Habakkuk and Jeremiah. The message of Jeremiah appears to be capsulated in verse 4, "Return now from your evil ways and from your evil deeds" (cf. Jer. 18:11; 25:5; 35:15). The words "evil ways" and "evil deeds" reflect the awful depravity of the Judeans in Jeremiah's day (cf. Jer. 2:13; 3:1-2; 5:7-9, 19). But the people neither heard nor did they heed God's Word through the prophets.

In verses 5-6*a* Zechariah asks three rhetorical questions designed to encourage his listeners to respond to his message. The first question, "Your fathers, where are they?" served to remind the returned exiles that the judgments announced by the former prophets were literally fulfilled. Their forefathers, having been killed or exiled by the Babylonians, were no more. The second question, "And the prophets, do they live forever?" served to remind the listeners that there was a

---

2. *Theological Wordbook of the Old Testament,* ed. R. L. Harris, G. L. Archer, B. K. Waltke, s.v. *seba'ot,* by J. E. Hartley, 2: 750-51.

limited opportunity during which to respond to the prophet's message. Judgment is certain, and life is short. Don't pass up the opportunity to repent today!

The third question (v. 6a) asked by Zechariah served to remind the returned exiles that their forefathers were judged in accordance with the stipulations of the Mosaic covenant. The "words and statutes" must refer specifically to the cursings of the covenant found in Deuteronomy 28:15-68. The same Hebrew word "overtake" occurs in Deuteronomy 28:15, 45 with reference to the curses that would overtake the disobedient Israelites as a savage beast overtakes its prey.

There is some debate as to whether the repentance referred to in verse 6b refers to the response of the former generation of Jews who had been taken into exile or to the later generation to whom Zechariah addressed his prophecies. The second view would be supported by the fact that the verb "repeated" in verse 6b is the same Hebrew word used in verse 3. Zechariah called the people to repentance (v. 3), and their response to his exhortation was immediate and positive. The antecedent of the *"they* repented" is found in verse 3, "therefore say to *them.*" Those who heard Zechariah returned to the Lord, "repented" as they had been exhorted in verse 3. In turning back to the Lord they acknowledged that the Lord's purpose had been accomplished in His dealings with their forefathers. The discipline of exile was in accordance with their evil ways and deeds (cf. 1:4). What had taken place in 586 B.C. was no mere chance happening. The destruction of Jerusalem was a manifestation of God's sovereign dealings with His disobedient people.

2

THE NIGHT VISIONS
OF ZECHARIAH

(ZECHARIAH 1:7—6:15)

Zechariah 1:7—6:15 contains a sequence of eight night visions followed by one symbolic action, the crowning of Joshua the high priest. These visions are reported by the prophet and explained by an interpreting angel. Whereas each vision may have originally functioned independently,[1] it is generally agreed that they are meant to be interpreted as a literary unit.

This section of Zechariah seems to pursue the same end as Haggai, that is, the rebuilding of the temple as the center of world rule and as a pilgrimage point for the nations (Zech. 8:20-23; Hag. 2:7-9).[2] The visions have their pivot or focus on the fifth vision (Zech. 4) in which the building of the Temple is central. Yet, as Baldwin points out, "Each contributes to the total picture of the role of Israel in the new era about to dawn."[3]

The question has been raised as to Zechariah's motive for publishing the visions and the symbolic coronation. H. G. May addressed himself to this issue some years ago, suggesting on the basis of the date (1:7) that Zechariah was planning on holding a secret coronation of Zerubbabel in the spring of

---

1. Brevard S. Childs, *Introduction to the Old Testament as Scripture* (Philadelphia: Fortress, 1979), p. 476.
2. W. J. Dumbrell, "Kingship and Temple in the Post-Exilic Period," 37 *The Reformed Theological Review* (May-August 1978): 39.
3. Joyce Baldwin, *Haggai, Zechariah, Malachi* (London: InterVarsity, 1972), p. 93.

the year.[4] According to May, this coronation was planned for New Year's Day, when Joshua the high priest would have also had a part in the ritual. He seeks to show that Zechariah drew his symbolism in chapter 3 from the mythological background of the New Year ritual he was familiar with in Babylonia.

Although that view remains an interesting possibility, it is based more on speculation than biblical data. The context of Zechariah suggests quite clearly that the prophecies were designed to call the people to repentance and to give comfort and encouragement to those in the throes of despair (1:12-17). It is speculative to suggest that Zechariah was trying to manipulate the people into accepting one whom he mistakenly identified as Messiah and was then forced to modify his message when his prophecies were not fulfilled. A more cautious approach to the visions is to let the interpreting angel speak for himself, recognizing that this section focuses on the centrality of the Temple and its rebuilding both as a challenge and an encouragement to the Jews of the restoration community.

THE RED HORSE RIDER AMONG THE MYRTLES (1:7-17)

Following the pattern of the Mesopotamian dream-visions, the first vision begins with a description of the setting. The vision was received on the twenty-fourth day of Shebat (January-February) in the second year of Darius, king of Persia, who ruled from 522 to 486 B.C. According to modern reckoning, the vision would be dated February 15, 519 B.C. The recipient of the vision was Zechariah the prophet, author of the book (1:1).

THE DESCRIPTION OF THE VISION (1:8)

The pattern in the visions of 1:7—6:15 is for Zechariah to describe what he saw ("I saw"), then ask the question "What

---

4. H. G. May, "A Key to the Interpretation of Zechariah's Visions," *Journal of Biblical Literature* 57 (1938): 173-84.

does this mean?'' and finally to have the explanation given
by the interpreting angel. In verse 8 Zechariah describes what
he saw in his first night vision. The fact that the vision took
place at night might lead one to conclude that the prophet was
dreaming. But that does not appear to be the case. He was
quite alert and actively involved in the visions both in observ-
ing and asking questions. The words ''I saw'' (1:8; cf. 1:18;
2:1; 3:1; 4:2) are used elsewhere of prophetic visions (Isa.
30:10; Gen. 41:22; Rev. 5:1; 7:1; 9:17).

In his first vision Zechariah observed a man riding on a red
horse standing among some myrtle trees in a ravine or deep
valley. Accompanying the rider on the red horse were troops
on red, sorrel, and white horses. The exact shade of color
meant by the unique Hebrew word translated ''sorrel'' is
uncertain. It is generally understood to mean a reddish
brown. After a thorough examination of the various possibil-
ities (''dappled,'' ''variegated,'' ''faint-colored, grey''), Gordon emends the text and suggests the translation ''white-
spotted''.[5] Although not mentioned specifically, it is quite
evident from the ''we'' of verse 11 that other riders are present. One other person is mentioned in connection with the vision—''the angel of the LORD'' to whom the riders report
(v. 11).

THE INTERPRETATION OF THE VISION (1:9-11)

Zechariah played a very active role in his night visions. In
verse 9 he asks the angel who acts as his guide and interpreter
throughout (1:18; 2:3; 4:1, 5; 5:5; 6:4), ''My lord, what are
these?'' The fact that Zechariah calls him ''lord'' does not
suggest that the angel is divine. The term is used frequently in
the Old Testament to refer to an earthly lord or master. It is
merely a respectful form of address. Note that the prophet
asks *what?* not *who?* He is interested in understanding the

---

5. R. P. Gordon, ''An Inner-Targum Corruption (Zech. I, 8)'' 25 *Vetus
   Testamentum* (April 1975): 216-19; see also Baldwin, *Haggai, Zechariah,
   Malachi,* pp. 138-40.

meaning of the vision, not just in identifying its participants. The angel promises to give the interpretation and does so by allowing Zechariah to overhear the words of those participating in the vision.

The man who was standing among the myrtles, apparently the leader of the riders and mounted on the red horse (v. 8), declared for Zechariah's benefit, "These are those whom the LORD has sent to patrol the earth" (v. 10) The word translated "patrol" in the NASB* literally means "walk to and fro." It suggests the idea of exploring or reconnoitering. In the time of Darius there was in the Persian administration an elaborate system of imperial inspectors known as the "King's Eyes and Ears." The inspectors went on annual circuits through the satrapies to investigate complaints and forestall disloyalty among the subjects.[6] As the Persian rulers used messengers on horseback to keep them informed on matters concerning the empire, so the Lord has patrollers to observe and report. That is not to suggest, however, that God *needs* someone to keep Him informed. In view of His omniscience, He knows all things (Ps. 147:4; Matt. 10:30).

In verse 11 "the angel of the LORD" is mentioned as standing among the myrtles. He is the one to whom the riders report. Some have sought to identify the "man" of verses 8 and 10 with the "angel" of verse 11. However, it is unlikely that the riders would report to someone who led them on their patrol. When the term "angel of the LORD" occurs with the definite article in the Old Testament, the context consistently indicates that the figure is a divine being (cf. Gen. 16:7, 13; Judg. 13:15-22). It is quite clear that *the* angel of the LORD is the second Person of the Trinity appearing in angelic form before His incarnation.[7]

---

*New American Standard Bible.

6. F. F. Bruce, *Israel and the Nations* (Grand Rapids: Eerdmans, 1963), p. 102.
7. H. C. Leupold, *Exposition of Zechariah* (Columbus, Ohio: Wartburg, 1956), p. 38.

The report received by the angel of the LORD was one of peace and quiet. "We have patrolled the earth, and behold, all the earth is peaceful and quiet" (v. 11). When Darius claimed the throne after the death of Cambyses in 522 B.C., the Persian Empire was in an upheaval. Many provinces were in revolt. A usurper, Gaumata, who pretended to be the brother of Cambyses, had seized the throne in an eastern region of the empire. Darius marched eastward into Media, captured Gaumata, and had him executed. During the next two years Darius defeated nine kings in nineteen battles to secure his throne. It was not until late in 520 B.C. that his position as king of Persia was actually secure. Peace had been established in the Persian Empire, but that was not necessarily good news for the Jews because they anticipated world upheavals to usher in the messianic age (Hag. 2:21-22).

THE MESSAGE ACCOMPANYING THE VISION (1:12-17)

The explanation of the vision is followed by a message of consolation for Israel. Having been disciplined through the exile, the Judeans will receive God's compassion (vv. 12, 16) and comfort (vv. 13, 17). The message also contains a promise that both Jerusalem and the Temple will be rebuilt (v. 16).

The angel of the LORD, who had received the patrol's report (v. 11), responded with a question, "O Yahweh of Hosts, how long will You have no compassion for Jerusalem and the cities of Judah, with which You have been indignant these seventy years?" (author's translation). Acting as intercessor for the returned exiles, the angel of Yahweh appeals to God regarding the continued humiliation of Jerusalem and the cities of Judah. The "seventy years" was the duration of exile and humiliation prophesied by Jeremiah (Jer. 25:11; 29:10). This is viewed as a period during which God showed His people "no compassion" (cf. Hos. 1:6). It is clear from verse 11 that the return to the land did not completely fulfill Jeremiah's prophecy. Jerusalem and the cities of Judah needed to be rebuilt. The "seventy years" may be calculated from

586 B.C., when the Jerusalem Temple was burned, to 515 B.C., when the Temple was rebuilt.[8]

The Lord's answer (v. 13) came not to the angel of the LORD, who had interceded on Jerusalem's behalf, but to the interpreting angel, who had been speaking to Zechariah (1:9). Yahweh responded with "gracious" (literally, "good") and "comforting" words. Zechariah may not have heard God reply personally. He received the divine message as communicated by the interpreting angel.

In verse 14 Zechariah is charged by the interpreting angel with proclaiming Yahweh's message (14b-17) to the people. The first statement of the oracle declares the basis for God's dealings with His people. "I am exceedingly jealous for Jerusalem and Zion." Yahweh is a jealous God (cf. Ex. 20:5; 34:14; Deut. 4:24).[9] The concept of jealousy is closely related to the emotions of anger and love. Because Yahweh is a jealous God He will tolerate no rivals or allow those who oppress His people to receive immunity from retribution. The terms *Jerusalem* and *Zion* can be used synonymously, but here they appear to refer to the city of Jerusalem (Ps. 48:2, 11-12) and the Temple area (Isa. 8:18).

Yahweh's anger (an aspect of His jealousy), is seen in verse 15 to be directed against the "nations." These nations are "at ease." They are complacent and feel secure when they should not feel so. Why? Because their retribution is due. Yahweh was "only a little angry" with His people. He wanted to discipline them, not destroy them. But the nations—the instruments of God's disciplinary judgment—took matters into their own hands and exceeded the limits of divine discipline. They literally "helped for evil." In their attacks on Judah and Jerusalem, the nations of Assyria, Babylon, and Edom overstepped their limits and caused evil to result. The Lord implies here and declares elsewhere that they will be held ac-

---

8. J. Carl Laney, *Ezra-Nehemiah* (Chicago: Moody, 1982), p. 46.
9. For a helpful note on divine jealousy, see Baldwin, *Haggai, Zechariah, Malachi,* pp. 101-3.

countable for their excesses (cf. 1:18-21; Jer. 51:10-24; Hab. 2:6-20).

In verse 16 Yahweh promises to "return to Jerusalem with compassion." This is reminiscent of Ezekiel's vision of the departure of the glory of Yahweh from the Temple and city (Ezek. 10:18-19, 11:23). God's return to Jerusalem will be accompanied by a display of His compassion. The attribute of "compassion" is the first mentioned in Yahweh's self revelation to Moses in Exodus 34:6-7. The word is related to the Hebrew term for "womb" and speaks of a motherly affection or tender sympathy (cf. Jer. 21:7).

Yahweh's compassion will be evidenced in four ways (vv. 16b-17). First, God's "house" (the Jerusalem Temple) will be rebuilt. Second, the city of Jerusalem will be reconstructed. The "measuring line" refers to an instrument used by a surveyor to establish boundaries and fix locations in preparation for building (cf. 2:1-2). The stretching out of a measuring line is the first step in the rebuilding of Jerusalem from the 586 B.C. Babylonian destruction. Third, the cities of Judah will be restored to prosperity. The promise of renewal is extended to all the cities that had been ravaged by the Babylonians. The expression "overflow" is used in Proverbs 5:16 for a spring that forcibly sends water out in all directions. So will the cities of Judah overflow with "prosperity" (literally, "good") as a result of God's compassionate dealings. Fourth, Zion will receive comfort, and Jerusalem will once again be the city of God's choice. The comfort promised Zion is reminiscent of God's words to Isaiah "Comfort, O comfort, My people" (Isa. 40:1). God's choice of Jerusalem is bound up with the presence of the Temple (1 Kings 8:44, 48; 2 Chron. 6:6, 34, 38) and is a prominent theme in Zechariah (1:17; 2:12; 3:2).

The first vision of Zechariah declares in essence that the nations are at peace. The accompanying message reveals that God will use this period of tranquility to manifest His compassion by restoring Jerusalem, the Temple, and the cities of Judah to prosperity. This vision is preparatory for those that

follow. It appears to "set the stage for subsequent vision."[10]
The message reflects God's attributes of compassion, jealousy, faithfulness, and sovereignty.

THE FOUR HORNS AND FOUR CRAFTSMEN (1:18-21)

Zechariah's second night vision focuses on "four horns"
and "four craftsmen." The vision contains a message of
judgment on the enemies of Judah.

THE FOUR HORNS (1:18-19)

The second vision is introduced by the words "Then I lifted
up my eyes," the common formula for introducing new visions. In his vision Zechariah sees four horns. Some have
speculated that the horns were attached to bulls that could not
be seen because of their grazing in tall grass. It is both fruitless and unwise to add to the vision to make it more understandable. Apocalyptic literature is noted for its enigma and
mystery. The "horns" refer to the hard, bonelike growths
projecting from the head of various hoofed animals including
oxen, sheep, and goats (cf. Gen. 22:13). Certain animals use
their horns as weapons to defend themselves or to attack an
intruder. The breaking of an animal's horn insures its defeat.
In light of this background, the horn is often used metaphorically in Scripture as a symbol of power and strength. To "cut
off" or "shatter" someone's horn means to bring about his
defeat (Ps. 75:10; Jer. 48:25; Dan. 8:7).

In response to his request for the interpretation of the vision, the angel informs Zechariah, "These are the horns
which have scattered Judah, Israel, and Jerusalem." Because
horns are associated with invincible strength, they are used in
the vision to represent powerful nations. "Scattered" is used
elsewhere of the scattering of God's people through exile
(1 Kings 14:15; Ezek. 6:8; 36:19). The horns, then, represent

10. William S. LaSor, D. A. Hubbard, F. W. Bush, *Old Testament Survey*
(Grand Rapids: Eerdmans, 1982), p. 496.

nations that have defeated and dispersed the people of Israel.

Various attempts have been made to identify the nations represented by the horns. The church Fathers regarded them as Assyria, Babylonia, Media, and Persia. Jerome preferred Babylonia, Medo-Persia, Greece, and Rome. Charles Feinberg follows that approach identifying the nations with the four empires of Daniel 2 and 7, namely, Babylonia, Medo-Persia, Greece, and Rome.[11] A more cautious approach is to avoid identifying the nations because the interpreting angel does not. The number "four" may be used to represent "the totality of opposition," as it appears to represent all directions in the eighth vision (6:1-8).[12]

THE FOUR CRAFTSMEN (1:20-21)

After viewing the four horns, Zechariah saw four craftsmen. The word "craftsman" or "smith" is used in the Old Testament of any sort of stoneworker, carpenter, or metalworker (Ex. 28:11; 1 Sam. 13:19, 2 Kings 12:12). In verse 21 Zechariah questions the interpreting angel, "What are these coming to do?" The question implies some anticipated activity. The angel explains that the craftsmen will intervene in behalf of Judah. The oppression of Judah is such that "no man lifts up his head," a figure of dejection and discouragement.

First, the craftsmen will "terrify" or "startle" the horns. The verb suggests a response of fear that manifests itself by trembling. Second, the craftsmen will defeat and subdue the horns of the nations. The phrase "horns of the nations" simply refers to the nations that the horns represent. The nations destined for defeat are further identified as those who "lift up their horns against the land of Judah" for the purpose of scattering the people. To "lift up" one's horn in such a manner is a sign of arrogance (cf. Ex. 14:8) similar to the sin

11. Charles L. Feinberg, *God Remembers: A Study of Zechariah,* 4th ed. (Portland, Ore.: Multnomah, 1979), p. 31-32.
12. Baldwin, *Haggai, Zechariah, Malachi,* p. 104.

of the "high hand" in the Hebrew text of Numbers 15:30 (NASB, "defiantly").

The second night vision of Zechariah is clearly a word of encouragement for the people of Judah. The enemies of God's people will be destroyed. Like the horns, the craftsmen represent powerful nations, perhaps even those nations opposed to Israel and Judah. The nations (the "horns") that have put Judah to flight will be overthrown and defeated by succeeding agents of destruction (the "craftsmen"). The vision reflects the sovereignty of God over the nations (Dan. 4:17, 35). It also displays both His power and authority to execute retribution (Deut. 32:35; Rom. 12:19).

THE SURVEYOR WITH A MEASURING LINE (2:1-13)

Zechariah's third night vision contains God's promise to restore Jerusalem and protect the city by His personal presence. It repeats the major theme and emphasis of the first vision but advances the thought a great deal further (cf. 2:4, 11). The first verse in the English translation corresponds to 2:5 in the Hebrew text.

THE VISION OF THE SURVEYOR (2:1-2)

This vision begins as did the previous one, "Then I lifted up my eyes" (2:1). Zechariah observes a man with a "measuring line" in his hand. Such an instrument was mentioned in the second vision, in which it was predicted that Jerusalem and the Temple would be rebuilt (1:16). Establishing boundaries and taking measurements are the first steps in any building project. The significance of the measuring line must have been obvious to Zechariah from the previous vision for he does not question the activity but rather asks "where" it would be performed (2:2). The man with the measuring line (not the interpreting angel) responds that he is going "to measure Jerusalem, to see how wide and how long it is." His apparent intent is to begin the rebuilding of the city by raising up its fortifications. Certainly it would be unwise to rebuild the Temple while the city was defenseless.

THE MESSAGE OF THE ANGEL (2:3-5)

In verse 3 Zechariah's interpreting angel encounters another angel—one apparently with greater authority. The second angel charges the interpreting angel with the task of delivering God's message to the man with the measuring line. The same Hebrew verb ("went forth") is used to describe the activity of both angels. Because they meet, it must be assumed that they "went forth" from different points of reference or, as Leupold says, "from opposite sides of the stage."[13]

The message to be delivered to the young man concerns the fact that despite its defenseless situation, Jerusalem will be inhabited by a multitude of men and cattle (2:4). The words "without walls" translate a Hebrew word that speaks of "open villages" as might be found in a rural district of Judea. Yet even without defensive fortifications, the inhabitants of Jerusalem will be secure. Their safety and security is grounded on the fact of God's personal presence in the city. Yahweh declares, "For I will be a wall of fire around her, and I will be the glory in her midst" (2:5).

Divine protection as a "wall of fire" is reminiscent of the protection offered by the pillar of cloud that stood between the camp of Israel and the camp of the Egyptians at the Red Sea (Ex. 14:19-20). The "pillar of cloud" and "pillar of fire" imagery is appropriated by Isaiah to describe the glorious protection provided for the inhabitants of Jerusalem in the messianic kingdom (Isa. 4:5). The promise that Yahweh will be "the glory in her midst" also has its background in the Exodus (Ex. 40:34). The glory that Ezekiel envisioned as departing (Ezek. 9:3; 10:19; 11:23) would be restored to Jerusalem by the personal presence of Yahweh (cf. Ezek. 43:2-5).

---

13. Leupold, *Exposition of Zechariah,* p. 54.

Whereas the first vision reveals that Jerusalem and the Temple would be rebuilt, the third vision guarantees God's protective presence for the inhabitants. This would be a great encouragement to the returned exiles as they contemplated the ruins of Jerusalem's defensive fortifications—a situation that Nehemiah was to resolve approximately seventy-five years later.

THE FUTURE OF JERUSALEM (2:6-13)

The rest of the chapter contains two exhortations. Each begins with an introductory command (vv. 6, 10) that is followed by an explanation ("for") and the prophet's comment ("Then you will know"). The first exhortation deals with the judgment on Israel's enemies and builds on the second vision. The second exhortation deals with the presence of God in Zion and builds on the third vision.[14]

The judgment on Israel's enemies (2:6-9). The first exhortation begins with an exclamation ("Ho there!) and is addressed to the Jews yet in exile. They are exhorted by Yahweh Himself to "flee from the land of the north" (v. 6)—an obvious reference to Babylon, the land of exile. It is interesting that they would have to be exhorted to leave after the decree of Cyrus gave them permission to do so. Josephus provides some insight here. He writes that many Jews did not want to leave Babylon on account of their possessions (*Antiquities* XI. 8).

The explanation ("for") acknowledges the fact that Yahweh sovereignly dispersed the disobedient Judeans, and thus He has the rightful authority to call for their return. The "four winds" is a metaphor (like the "four points of the compass") referring to the fact that the exiles were dispersed in all directions (cf. Matt. 24:31). Verse 7 repeats the essence of the exhortation, specifying further the addresses and their place of residence. As "Zion" represents the people of Zion,

14. Baldwin, *Haggai, Zechariah, Malachi,* pp. 107-8.

"daughter of Babylon" signifies the people of the realm of Babylon.

Verses 8 and 9 contain a message that confirms and amplifies the message of the second vision (1:18-21) that God will judge those who persecute His people, Israel. The first matter to be settled here is the identity of the individual Yahweh "sent." It could be a reference to Zechariah. Another possibility is that the one sent is the angel of the Lord. Yet that seems unlikely in a context where there is no mention of the angel of the Lord. Whereas scholarly opinion is divided on this matter, the immediate context suggests that the one sent is Zechariah the prophet.

A second difficult question is the meaning of the phrase "after glory" (v. 8). Those who view the one "sent" as the angel of the Lord understand the "glory" to refer to either Messiah's glorious appearing or the vindication of God's glory by Messiah's judgment on the nations. By taking the one "sent" as a reference to the prophet, it is possible to argue that the "glory" refers to Zechariah's vision. It is also possible to translate the phrase as "with glory" (cf. Ps. 73:24, NASB margin). Because the word "glory" is derived from the Hebrew word for "weight," Zechariah may simply be saying, "With a weighty burden Yahweh sent me to pronounce judgment against the nations that plunder Israel."

Carola J. L. Kloos argues rather convincingly that the phrase "after glory" has to do with the purpose of Zechariah's mission (i.e., "in order to obtain glory").[15] Ezekiel 39:21 provides a striking parallel in setting forth the thought of God's honor among the nations in the context of judgment. The thrust of verses 8 and 9 would then be, "Yahweh sent me to restore His honor, saying that He will punish the nations, and when He has done so, you shall know that Yahweh has indeed sent me."

15. Carola J. L. Kloos, "Zech. II 12: Really A Crux Interpretum?" *Vetus Testamentum* 25 (October 1975): 729-36.

Zechariah warns that the nation that would plunder God's people, Israel, "touches the apple (better, 'pupil') of His eye." The word "touches" in this context suggests "touching with intent to harm." Zechariah may have drawn that figure of speech from Deuteronomy 32:10. Because eyesight is so precious, those who would harm someone's eye subject themselves to the peril of severe retribution. According to God's covenant promise to Abraham, one cannot harm Israel without incurring the curse of divine judgment (Gen. 12:3). The fate of Haman in the book of Esther is a classic illustration of this principle.

Verse 9 contains the message of Yahweh concerning the destiny of Israel's plunderers. The returned exiles are encouraged with the promise of a reversal of positions so that the plunderers will be plundered by those who were their slaves. The "slaves" would refer to the Jews in captivity. Yahweh will accomplish this reversal by the mere wave of His hand—a gesture of sovereignty. It is clear that this is God's doing, not man's. The last line of verse 9, "then you will know!" contains the words of Zechariah. Like the prophets before him, the fulfillment of his prophecy will authenticate his commission as God's messenger (cf. Deut. 18:21-22).

The presence of God in Zion (2:10-13). The exhortation in verses 10-13 builds on the third vision (2:1-6). The people of Jerusalem are addressed as "daughter of Zion" (2:4, 5; 8:3) and implored to sing and rejoice. The reason for such rejoicing is Yahweh's promise, "I am coming and I will dwell in your midst" (2:10). It is from the verb "dwell" that the word *Shekinah* is derived. The verb "dwell" is used of the presence of God in the midst of Israel as represented by His "dwelling" in the Tabernacle (Ex. 25:8). Similarly, the Temple served as the place of God's dwelling among His people (1 Kings 6:13). With the destruction of the Temple in 586 B.C. Jerusalem lost the visible reminder of God's invisible presence, although Ezekiel envisioned Yahweh's departure before the Temple's actual destruction (Ezek. 9:3; 10:19; 11:23). The rebuilding of the Temple, then underway (Ezra

5:1-2), would have been an encouragement to the returned ex-iles that Yahweh would again manifest His personal presence among His people (cf. Ex. 29:45). The incarnation of Jesus the Messiah may have been the initial realization of this promise (cf. John 1:14). However, Christ's coming in glory to rule His kingdom will bring the prophecy to its ultimate fulfillment.

The personal presence of God in Jerusalem will make it a center for pilgrimage and worship (2:11). Many *goyim* ("Gentile nations") will "join themselves" with Yahweh in that day and become His people. The words "My people" are used frequently in the context of the renewal of God's cove-nant with His believing people (Jer. 31:33; 32:38; Hos. 2:23). The transition from many nations to one people of God is very important to the theology of Paul (Eph. 2:11-16, 19; 3:6). When will this great day of pilgrimage and worship occur? Isaiah anticipated its fulfillment in the coming kingdom when Messiah will rule and reign from Jerusalem (Isa. 2:2-3; 14:1-2; cf. Mic. 4:1-2).

The last phrase in verse 11 ("then you will know," NEB*) is best understood as the words of Zechariah. This statement is set in balance with the almost identical words of verse 9. The fulfillment of this prophecy will serve to confirm the fact that Zechariah was divinely commissioned.

Not only will God in the future dwell among His people, but verse 12 reveals that He will again possess Judah as His inheritance. "Judah" refers here to the people of Judah rather than to the tribal territory (cf. Deut. 32:10). The familiar phrase "the holy land" occurs only here in the Hebrew Bible. The election of Jerusalem, a prominent theme in the message accompanying the first vision (1:16), appears again here. Jerusalem will be God's choice as the center for worship, religious instruction, and judicial decision during the messianic kingdom (Isa. 2:1-4).

Verse 13 contains a final exhortation that appears to be

New English Bible.

based on the two messages accompanying the third vision (2:6-9 and 2:10-12). Because God is coming to judge the nations and establish His rule in Jerusalem, all mankind ("flesh") is called to be hushed in awesome reverence and respect (cf. Rev. 8:1). Unlike Habakkuk who declared that "the LORD [Yahweh] is in His holy temple" (Hab. 2:20), Zechariah declares that Yahweh has departed from his heavenly sanctuary. The word "aroused" suggests that He is about to commence His prophesied activity (cf. 4:1).

The vision of chapter 3 is designed to encourage the returned exiles that God has not set aside Jerusalem or His people. In spite of its defenseless situation, the city would be restored and protected by God Himself. He promises, in addition, to reverse the fortunes of those who plundered Israel and to dwell in the midst of His believing people.

THE CLEANSING OF JOSHUA THE HIGH PRIEST (3:1-10)

The fourth vision of Zechariah is different from the previous three in that the angel simply presents the vision without offering any interpretation. The significance of the action is explained by the participants as the vision is revealed. The symbolic cleansing of Joshua the high priest depicts the cleansing of God's people by the work of Messiah. Verses 1-5 contain one of the best biblical illustrations of the imputation of righteousness (cf. Rom. 5:17; 2 Cor. 5:21).

THE SYMBOLIC ACTION (3:1-5)

Like the prologue of Job, the vision has its setting in a heavenly courtroom. Three figures are observed in this scene. Zechariah is shown "Joshua the high priest standing before the angel of the LORD, and Satan standing at his right hand to accuse him" (3:1). As high priest, Joshua (also spelled Jeshua, Ezra 5:2; Hag. 1:12), the son of Jozadak, held the highest religious office in the restoration community. Two important observations need to be made about the high priest. First, he was to be the very essence of purity. Under no circumstances was he to become defiled or unclean (Lev. 21:10-15). Second, the high priest bore the names of the twelve tribes on his breastplate (Ex. 28:29) and thus represented the people of Israel before God. Also in the heavenly courtroom is the angel of the LORD, the preincarnate Christ, who represents Yahweh in the deliberations. The third figure is Satan, whose name is a transliteration of the Hebrew word for "adversary" or "accuser." Satan (literally, "the accuser") serves as a prosecuting attorney before God's tribunal (cf. Job 1:6-10; Rev. 12:10). Christ, his heavenly counterpart, serves as the believers' advocate, or counsel for the defense (1 John 2:1).

The charges being brought against Joshua are not specified. Jewish tradition suggests that Joshua was guilty due to his son's intermarriage with foreign wives (Ezra 10:18). But how could Joshua be responsible for sins his sons committed a generation later? It is probable that the accusation is not directed against Joshua as an individual, but rather as a representative of the Jewish people in need of spiritual cleansing.[16]

In verse 2 Satan the accuser is twice rebuked by the "LORD," an abbreviated reference to the angel of the LORD (3:1). The rebuke is administered by the authority of Yahweh ("The LORD rebuke you, Satan!"). This is not to suggest that the angel of Yahweh, the preincarnate Christ, is less than divine. While coequal in the Godhead, the Son submits to the authority of the Father (1 Cor. 11:3; Phil. 2:5-8). The repetition of the rebuke is for emphasis. The theme of God's choice of Jerusalem is highlighted in the second rebuke (cf. 1:17; 2:12; 3:2). God's choice of Jerusalem guarantees the protection of the city and people.

The rebuke of Satan concludes with a strongly worded rhetorical question, "Is this not a brand plucked from the

---

16. Eli Cashdan, "Zechariah," in *The Twelve Prophets,* ed. A. Cohen (London: Soncino, 1948), p. 280.

fire?'' The figure recalls the reference of the prophet Amos to
the Northern Kingdom of Israel as a "firebrand snatched
from a blaze" (Amos 4:1). Similar imagery is used with
reference to Israel's deliverance from the Egyptian captivity
(Deut. 4:20; Jer. 11:4). Snatching a burning branch from the
fire would deliver it from complete destruction. Through the
return decreed by Cyrus, God has plucked Joshua and a
precious remnant of His people from the "furnace" of exile.
The rhetorical question implies that the God who delivered
His people will certainly protect and defend them against
Satan's attacks.

Verse 3 reveals that Joshua was clothed in "filthy
garments" as he stood before the angel of the Lord. According to Exodus 28:2 the garments of the high priest were to be
"holy"—set apart from secular use. They were to add glory
and beauty to the priestly office and ritual. Those splendid
vestments included the ephod, breastplate of judgment, robe,
golden headplate, turban, tunic, and sash (Ex. 28:4, 6-39).
The adjective translated "filthy" occurs only here and in the
following verse and suggests the most vile of conditions. It
literally means "befouled with excrement." Whereas the high
priest's garments were to be most holy, Joshua's garments are
seen to be soiled beyond imagination. How could sin from
God's viewpoint be more graphically and dramatically por-
trayed?

As Joshua stands before the angel of the Lord, quite helpless to remedy his own condition, the angel issues a command. Addressing some angelic assistants awaiting His command ("standing before him") He declares, "Remove the
filthy garments from him" (3:4). That the filthy garments are
removed for Joshua indicates that he is unable to cleanse
himself. The angel of the Lord then explains the symbolic action. "See, I have taken your iniquity away from you and will
clothe you with festal robes." Joshua's soiled garments are
representative of the defilement of sin. The word "iniquity"
is derived from a verb that means "to bend" or "to twist"
and suggests a perversion or twisting aside from what is right.

It is sometimes used of the guilt or punishment incurred as a result of sin.

The removal of Joshua's iniquity is a picture of what God is able to accomplish for His people Israel, whom Joshua represents, and for all those burdened with the guilt of sin. He does not just remove those soiled garments and leave them around as reminders of our past. Rather, as David declares, "As far as the east is from the west, so far has He removed our transgressions from us" (Ps. 103:12).

The cleansing of Joshua is not completed with the mere removal of his sin-soiled garments. Another step is necessary—the provision of fresh, new clothes. Joshua is told by the angel of the LORD that He will be clothed with "festal robes" (3:4). The new garments are not only clean (3:5), they are richly appointed—the kind usually reserved for special occasions. As an active participant in the council of Yahweh on this crucial occasion, Zechariah joins in the proceedings: "Let them put a clean turban on his head" (3:5).[17] His suggestion is apparently the wish of the angel of Yahweh "standing by." Joshua is immediately clothed with festal robes and crowned with a clean turban. The word "turban" refers to a cloth wound about the head. Because this is a related word (but not the exact word used) for the high priest's turban (Ex. 28:4, 29), one should not be dogmatic in suggesting that Joshua was clothed in high priestly attire. But the point of the vision is clear. As representative of the people, Joshua stood before God clothed in iniquity. His cleansing represents the graciousness of Yahweh in being both able and willing to remove the guilt and defilement of the people of Judah.

What better picture is there of the doctrine of the imputation of righteousness to the believer? As sin is removed by the person and work of Christ, so the very righteousness of Christ

---

17. For a study of the implications of Zechariah's participation in the proceedings, see N. L. A. Tidwell, *"Wa'omar* (Zech. 3:5) and the Genre of Zechariah's Fourth Vision," *Journal of Biblical Literature* (September 1975): 343-55.

is placed on the believer's account (Rom. 5:18-19; 2 Cor. 5:21). That this is accomplished completely by grace is demonstrated by the fact that Joshua had no part in his cleansing. He simply received the clean garments as the believer receives the righteousness of Christ apart from any meritorious activity (Gal. 2:16).

THE PROPHETIC ADMONITION (3:6-10)

The remainder of chapter 3 records a prophetic admonition given by the angel of the Lord to Joshua the high priest. Some have argued that the admonition is meant for Joshua personally and that he is promised reward at his resurrection in return for his obedience and faithfulness. Others have suggested that in these verses Joshua is representative of Jesus, the Messiah, who is the believer's faithful high priest. Still others understand that Joshua is presenting the people of Israel as he clearly did in the preceding symbolic action. That third view is preferred because it has the definite advantage of consistency. As Joshua represented the people of Israel in cleansing from iniquity, so he represents the people in God's promise of future blessing for obedience.

After the climactic crowning of Joshua, the angel of the LORD solemnly charged the high priest regarding his future ministry. The appeal to "the Lord of hosts" (3:7) adds a heightened measure of authority to the charge. The charge is composed of two conditions ("if") and three promises ("then"). The first condition ("if you will walk in My ways") suggests complete conformity to God's revealed will. The word *walk* is used throughout Scripture as a metaphor of living or carrying on one's activities. The charge "to walk in God's ways" is used frequently in Deuteronomy in the sense of keeping the covenant (Deut. 8:6; 10:12; 11:22; 19:9). The second condition, "And if you will perform My service" suggests the faithful observance of Joshua's worship responsibilities, specifically that of the Temple ritual. The word *serve* is used elsewhere of religious obligations to be observed (Num. 3:7, 25).

Three blessings are promised if the two conditions are met. First, the Lord tells Joshua that he will "govern My house." The "house" may refer to the Temple, in which case the first two blessings would be almost identical. On the other hand, it may refer to the Jewish people as the "house of Israel" (1 Chron. 28:4; cf. Gen. 12:1; 2 Sam. 7:16). The word *rule* means "to judge" and suggests the exercise of judicial functions. Whereas the first promise relates to Joshua's authority in relationship to the people, the second relates to his authority in relationship to the Temple ("My courts"). For his faithfulness, Joshua is promised the privilege of exercising authority over the Temple and its courts. That was a very special promise because since the destruction of the Temple nearly seventy years before, no high priest had exercised such authority.

The third promise given Joshua as representative of God's people is that of "free access among those who are standing here." Those "standing" by must refer to God's angels who assisted in the removal of Joshua's garments (3:4). The "free access" (v. 7) promised could not refer to access to the Temple, for Joshua had that right by virtue of his priestly office. Access "among" the angels is probably a respectful way of referring to direct communion with God. As the angels have access to the throne of God, so Joshua would be standing among them, sharing in the privilege of direct communion with God.

It seems rather clear from both the context (3:2, 9) and the concept of the high priest that Joshua serves to represent the people of Judah. The promises given to him are no doubt the special favors God's people will enjoy as they are faithful to His covenant. Having been cleansed and converted, the nation of Israel will fulfill its destiny to be all that Joshua represents—a kingdom of priests and a holy nation (Ex. 19:6).

In verses 8-10 Joshua and his associates are addressed by the Lord Himself. That the speaker is God is indicated by verse 10 ("declares the LORD of hosts") and the use of the first person ("I am going to bring in My Servant"). The words "Now listen" (v. 8) indicate that the message that follows is of special importance. Joshua's "friends" who are sitting before him must be his priestly associates (v. 10). God declares that they are "a symbol" (v. 8). The word is used elsewhere in the Old Testament for a sign or token of a future event. The prophet Ezekiel was a "sign" (Ezek. 12:6, 11) as were Isaiah and his children (Isa. 8:18). Precisely what Joshua and his associates signify is not revealed in the passage. It has been suggested that they symbolize the priestly ministry of Israel in the future day when the nation is cleansed and converted.[18] That view would be in keeping with the representative nature of the priesthood in this vision.

God promises "to bring in My Servant the Branch." It would be difficult to miss the obvious reference to the messianic Servant in Isaiah's servant songs (Isa. 42:1-9; 49:1-12; 50:4-9; 52:12—53:13). The word *Branch* (or "shoot") is used to further identify God's Servant. Isaiah uses a similar term to refer to Messiah, who will "spring from the stem of Jesse" as a tender sprout shoots up from the ground (Isa. 11:1; 4:2; 53:2). More is revealed concerning the person and work of the Branch in 6:12-13 (cf. Jer. 23:5; 33:15).

In verse 9 the Lord describes a stone that He has set before Joshua. The stone has "seven eyes" and will be engraved with an inscription. It has been suggested that the stone reflects the Mesopotamian practice of engraving the foundation stone of a new temple. Others argue that the ornamented stone is to crown the Temple structure. Luther's view that the stone represents the church has been followed by many. Other conservative scholars assert that the stone represents Christ. Each of those interpretations can be defended from other texts but involve some speculation in that the stone is not identified as any of those in this vision. Perhaps identifying the stone is not necessary to a proper understanding of the passage.

The stone is said to have "seven eyes." The word "eyes"

---

18. Merrill F. Unger, *Zechariah: Prophet of Messiah's Glory* (Grand Rapids: Zondervan, 1963), p. 64.

can also be translated "springs" or "fountains." Lipinski argues for that meaning here.[19] Like the rock in the wilderness (Ex. 17:6; Num. 20:7-11), the specially engraved stone brings forth a profusion of water that symbolizes the cleansing of the people (cf. 3:4). The Lord explains, "And I will remove the iniquity of the land in one day." Verses 8 and 9 unite to present a central theme. The bringing in of the Messiah ("the Branch") will result in the removal of the iniquity from the land. The cleansing of the land is representative of the spiritual cleansing to be accomplished by Messiah (13:1; cf. John 13:10b-11; 15:3). This view has the merit of simplicity and avoids speculation in attempting to identify the "stone." Whereas the "one day" has been taken by some to refer to the day of Christ's atoning work on Calvary, it may be better understood as that future day when God's people Israel appropriate the work of the cross by faith (12:10—13:1; Rom. 11:26-27).

Verse 10 depicts the physical prosperity that comes as a result of Messiah's work. The phrase "in that day" is used throughout the Old Testament and frequently in Zechariah to refer to the Day of the Lord. Here it refers to a particular aspect of that day that is characterized by prosperity and blessing. It is undoubtedly a reference to the messianic era (14:20-21). Sitting under one's vine and a fig tree is a proverbial description of prosperity and contentment (1 Kings 4:25; Isa. 36:16). Micah used this imagery to depict the conditions of the future messianic kingdom (Mic. 4:4).

THE LAMPSTAND AND TWO OLIVE TREES (4:1-14)

The fifth vision of Zechariah relates to the completion of the Temple (4:9). It was designed to serve both as a corrective and an encouragement for Zerubbabel that the rebuilding of the Temple would be accomplished not by human ingenuity but by divine power.

19. E. Lipinski, "Recherches sur le Livre de Zecharie," *Vetus Testamentum* 20 (1970): 25-29.

THE DESCRIPTION OF THE LAMPSTAND (4:1-3, 12)

In verse 1 Zechariah is prepared by the interpreting angel for another vision. There is no clear indication in the original text that the angel had left the prophet. When coordinated with a second verb ("roused"), "returned" may simply mean "again" (i.e., "he roused me again"). And it is not necessary to view Zechariah as having fallen asleep in the ordinary sense of the word. He was roused "*as* a man who is awakened from his sleep." As a man is roused from sleep, the prophet was alerted to receive yet another vision.

In response to the angel's question, "What do you see?" Zechariah describes a golden lampstand standing between two olive trees (4:2-3). It has been assumed by many that the lampstand described is essentially the same as the seven-branched lampstand of the Tabernacle (Ex. 25:31-40). They liken Zechariah's lampstand to the menorah depicted on the arch of Titus in Rome. Archaeological investigation has shed considerable light on the discussion of what Zechariah saw.[20]

The lampstand that Zechariah saw was probably more of a cylindrical pedestal that flared slightly at the top. An unusual feature of this lampstand was that it was of gold rather than pottery. On top of the pedestal was a "curved thing" usually identified as a bowl, although it has been thought by some to refer to the flaring feature at the top of the column (cf. 1 Kings 7:41). On top of the "curved thing" were seven lamps, each with seven spouts. Bowl-shaped lamps of the biblical period generally had a pinch at the rim of the bowl, which was suited for holding a wick. The seven lamps that Zechariah saw had seven pinches ("spouts") each. A bowl lamp dated c. 900 B.C. found at the site of Dan is very similar to the one in Zechariah's vision. It sets on a pedestal and has seven pinches, or flutes, for seven wicks.[21]

The two olive trees that stand to the right and the left of the

20. Robert North, "Zechariah's Seven-Spout Lampstand," *Biblica* 51 (1970): 183-206.
21. Ibid. See the plate opposite page 192 in North's article.

lampstand are further described in verse 12. Zechariah questions the interpreting angel about the "two olive branches" and "two golden pipes." "Branches" may be better translated "clusters" and suggests that the tree was heavily laden with fruit. The word "pipes" occurs only here in the Old Testament, and its meaning is debated. Yet the idea of "pipes" or "funnels" fits well in this context. They served as channels for the "gold." This is undoubtedly a reference to the olive oil, which is yellow in color, hence "golden oil."

After viewing the vision of the golden lampstand between the two olive trees, Zechariah asks the interpreting angel the meaning of the vision. "What are these, my lord?" (v. 4). It has been suggested that the prophet's question was only with reference to the two olive trees (vv. 11-12). But the general nature of the angel's response (vv. 6-10) indicates that Zechariah was interested in the overall meaning of the vision. Later he asks for some specific details (vv. 11-12). The angel responded to Zechariah's inquiry by questioning, "Do you not know what these are?" (v. 5). The interpreting angel does not appear to be suggesting that Zechariah should have been able to determine the meaning of the vision on his own. Rather he seems to be emphasizing the prophet's inability to know the meaning without divine interpretation. The delay serves to heighten the suspense and focus the prophet's (and the reader's) attention on the angel's words.

Rather than interpreting the details of the vision, the interpreting angel gives Zechariah a message for Zerubbabel, the governor of Judah (Hag. 2:1). It is noteworthy that as the previous vision focused on Joshua the high priest, the message of the fifth vision focuses on Zerubbabel. The fact that there were two leaders in the restoration community— one religious and one civil—is helpful in understanding the explanation of the olive trees in verses 11-14.

Recent scholarship has argued that Zechariah 4:6-10 must be understood in light of ancient Near Eastern texts depicting the ritual for rededicating temples.[22] According to this view-point, Zechariah is depicted in the vision as a royal partici-pant in the ritual rededication of the restoration Temple. Although there is some merit to this approach, it would be well to exercise caution because the evidence for such ritual is fragmentary and based on Mesopotamian rather than Israel-ite worship. It is questionable that the returned exiles of the restoration community who were so diligent to preserve the sanctity of the worship center (Ezra 4:1-4) would have risked contamination by involving themselves in Mesopotamian temple ritual.

The succinct message to Zerubbabel in verse 6 contains the key to understanding the fifth vision. "Not by might nor by power, but by My Spirit," declares the LORD of hosts. The re-building of the Temple, which had begun again in earnest (Ezra 5:1-2; Hag. 1:14), would be accomplished not by human strength or resources but by the power of God's Spirit. The close connection with the preceding vision and this promise is readily apparent. As the lamp was fed with oil without human effort, so the Temple will be restored not by the strength or ingenuity of Zerubbabel, but by the power and provision of God.

Verse 7 applies the lesson of verse 6 to the experience of Zerubbabel. A "great mountain" is personified and ad-dressed. "Before Zerubbabel you will become a plain." Elsewhere in Scripture, mountains sometimes represent obstacles or difficulties (Isa. 40:4; Matt. 17:20). There were plenty of such mountainous obstacles facing the builders of the restoration Temple (Ezra 4:1-4; 5:3-5). Such obstructions would "become a plain," that is, unable to hinder God's work. It is said of Zerubbabel that he will bring forth the "top stone" (literally, "head stone"). Some have argued on

---

22. David L. Petersen, "Zerubbabel and Jerusalem Temple Reconstruction," *Catholic Biblical Quarterly* 36 (July 1974): 366-72; Baruch Halpern, "The Ritual Background of Zechariah's Temple Song," *Catholic Biblical Quarterly* 40 (April 1978): 167-90.

the basis of analogy with Mesopotamian temple dedication ritual that this must refer to the foundation stone. The historical setting of the book, however, reveals that the foundation has already been laid (Ezra 3:1-10). What is yet anticipated is the completion of the work (4:9). Setting the "top stone" as the culmination of the building project would be most appropriate. This final act by Zerubbabel is to be accompanied by shouts, "Grace, grace to it!" That may be understood either as a prayer for God's favor to rest upon the Temple or as a cry of admiration over the grace or beauty it possesses.

Verses 8 and 9 advance further the message of verse 7. Zechariah is told by the Lord that as Zerubbabel laid the foundation of the Temple, so his hands will finish the work. Verse 9 does not just repeat the thought of verse 7 that the Temple will be completed but emphasizes the certainty and immediacy of the fulfillment of the event. As in 2:9 and 11, the fulfillment of the prophecy in the prophet's lifetime will confirm the fact that Zechariah truly speaks for Yahweh.

Verse 10 contains further encouragement for Zerubbabel. There were those in the restoration community who remembered the Temple of Solomon in all its splendor and glory. They could not help making a comparison with the smaller, not so magnificent, restoration Temple. The second Temple seemed "like nothing" when compared with the first (Hag. 2:3). The rhetorical question in verse 10 contains a rebuke to those who would "despise the day of small things." There is nothing wrong with a small work. Little is much if God is in it.

The rest of verse 10 bristles with difficulties. Who or what are the "seven"? What is the meaning of the words translated "plumb line"? What are the "eyes" of the Lord? Most commentators take the "seven" to refer to the lamps mentioned in verse 3. Another possibility, however, is that the "seven" refers back to the "eyes" ("springs") mentioned in the admonition to Joshua in 3:9. It has already been seen that the fourth and fifth visions complement each other and should be

taken together. Yet the nearest antecedent and least com-
plicated approach would point toward identifying the
"seven" with the "seven lamps."

The words "plumb line" may be literally translated "the
stone of tin." This is not the usual expression for "plumb
line" (cf. Amos 7:7-8) and has led to the suggestion that the
stone symbolizes separation as tin must be separated from
ore. The stone would then symbolize the separated nature of
the Jewish community. But how could this be "in the hand of
Zerubbabel" (v. 10)? In keeping with the view that this
passage reflects Mesopotamian dedication ritual, it has also
been suggested that the "stone of tin" was a tin tablet
deposited in the foundation of the Temple. Tablets of this
sort, though usually of silver or gold, have been found in
archaeological excavations. However, it is clear from verse 9
that the foundation has already been laid. The idea of a
"plumb line" fits well with the thought of building (4:7, 9),
which is clearly the thrust of the immediate context.

The seven "eyes of the LORD" have been related by some
to the seven "eyes" on the stone mentioned in 3:9. However,
it has been pointed out earlier that the "eyes" of 3:9 are better understood as springs. It is better to work within the immediate context of the fifth vision ("these seven") and identify the seven eyes with the "seven lamps" (4:2). Used sym-
bolically, the number seven represents the idea of complete-
ness (cf. Gen. 2:1-3). The seven "eyes of the LORD which
range to and fro throughout the earth" reflect His omniscience. The fact that these eyes will be glad when they see the
plumb line in Zerubbabel's hand suggests the delight of God
over the rebuilding of the Jerusalem Temple.

Verses 11-14 provide further information into the meaning
and significance of the fifth vision. Zechariah asks the interpreting angel to explain the two olive trees on either side of
the lampstand (v. 11). The request in verse 12 is more specific
and provides further details of what Zechariah saw. The
prophet wants to know the meaning of the two olive branches
or "clusters" that empty their golden oil into the two golden

pipes. The "golden pipes" apparently transfer the oil from the clusters to the seven lamps so that they are able to burn continually and without human assistance.

The question asked by the interpreting angel, "Do you not know what these are?" (4:13) prepares the way for the final revelation to Zechariah regarding the meaning of the fifth vision. The prophet is told, "These are the two anointed ones, who are standing by the Lord of the whole earth" (4:14).

The expression "anointed ones" is literally "sons of oil" and suggests the idea of anointing. The anointing of a king (1 Sam. 10:10; 16:13) or a priest (Ex. 30:30; Num. 7:1) was a religious act that set the individual apart as a special representative in relationship with Yahweh. The king represented Yahweh's rulership over the land and the people. The priest represented the people before the Lord. It is suggested by most commentators that the two anointed ones are Joshua the high priest and Zerubbabel the governor of Judah. But such specific identification is not provided in the text, nor is it essential to an understanding of its message (cf. Rev. 4:11). The two anointed ones would, however, probably represent the highest religious and political offices in Israel—king and high priest. The reference to the two "standing by the Lord" represents them in a position of service. They are servants of the Lord of the whole earth. It is through the two offices of king and priest realized in the servant Jesus Christ that the purposes of God for His people will be ultimately accomplished (cf. 6:12-13).

The fifth vision and the explanation that follows serves to encourage the restoration community by assuring the leaders and people that God would accomplish His purposes for them in spite of the mountainous obstacles they faced in rebuilding the Temple. God's purposes will be accomplished by His power, apart from human might or resources.

The Flying Scroll (5:1-4)

Zechariah's sixth and seventh visions deal with the subject of the wicked and ungodly in Israel. How are the disobedient to be dealt with? In these two visions Zechariah learns that not only will individual sinners be judged (5:1-4), but the principle of wickedness will be removed from among God's people (5:5-11).

THE SCROLL DESCRIBED (5:1-2)

Lifting up his eyes again, Zechariah beholds a "flying scroll" (5:1). A "scroll" was a rolled parchment, or vellum document, that corresponded in function to a book (cf. Jer. 36:1-8). In verse 2 the interpreting angel asks the prophet, "What do you see?" In response Zechariah describes the scroll as flying through the air, thus available for all to see and read. The dimensions of the scroll are 20 by 10 cubits, or 30 by 15 feet (a cubit being equal to eighteen inches).

It has been observed that the scroll has the same dimensions as the Holy Place in the Tabernacle (Ex. 26:15-28) and the porch of Solomon's Temple (1 Kings 6:3). Whereas some commentators have sought to find significance in this similarity, none is given by the interpreting angel in the explanation of the vision.

THE SCROLL EXPLAINED (5:3-4)

Verse 3 reveals that the scroll, like that seen by Ezekiel (Ezek. 2:10), had writing on both sides. The interpreting angel identifies the writing on the scroll as containing a message of judgment. "This is the curse that is going forth over the face of the whole land." The word "curse" is used in connection with the Mosaic covenant (Deut. 30:7). Through Moses God revealed that obedience to the stipulations of the covenant would result in blessings (Deut. 28:1-16), but disobedience would result in judgment or "cursings" (Deut. 27:15-26; 28:15-68). The message on the scroll is that the cursings of the covenant will be executed upon the whole land. The "land" is a figure of metonomy whereby the place named refers to those who occupy it (i.e., the inhabitants of the land). Whereas the designation may be understood in a broad sense (i.e., "the inhabitants of earth"), the context of the covenant would suggest specific application to the people of the land of Judah.

The latter part of verse 3 mentions two classes of evildoers as representative of those on whom the curse will be applied. The curse will fall upon "everyone who steals" and "everyone who swears." The one who "swears" is identified in verse 4 as swearing falsely in the name of God by using the name of God in an unholy and irreverent manner. Those who violate the third and eighth commandments (Ex. 20:7, 15) will be "purged away." The verb "purged away" bears the sense of removed from the covenant community. The method of removal is not revealed and could be either by exile (Deut. 28:63-64) or by death (Num. 15:30-31, 35-36).

Verse 4 reveals that the judgment of God on those who violate His covenant will be sure, penetrating, and severe. Yahweh declares in essence, "I will not fail to execute judgment on those who violate His will." Nor will the wicked find refuge, for the curse will enter into the very houses of the evildoers to accomplish its purpose. The severity of the judgment is evidenced by the words "It will spend the night within the house and consume it with its timbers and stones." This metaphor is reminiscent of the fire of Yahweh that fell on Elijah's altar consuming not only the offering but the wood, stones, dust, and water (1 Kings 18:38).

The sixth vision of Zechariah reveals that God will bring judgment where judgment is due. No one of the returned exiles could persist in disobedience and expect to escape the severe and penetrating wrath of God.

THE WOMAN IN THE EPHAH (5:5-11)

The seventh vision of Zechariah sets forth the message that sin will be permanently removed from the land of Israel. Although the exile had purged the Jewish people from idolatry, they had returned to the land where wickedness and false worship abounded (cf. 2 Kings 17:24-41; Ezra 4:1-5). As the sixth vision revealed that the wicked people would be purged from the land, the seventh vision reveals that the land itself will be purged of wickedness.

THE APPEARANCE OF THE EPHAH (5:5-8)

During the intervals between the visions, the interpreting angel falls into the background.[23] In verse 5 he again appears on the scene and commands Zechariah, "Lift up now your eyes, and see what this is, going forth." Zechariah asks the angel for a positive identification of the object he observes. He is told, "This is the ephah going forth" (v. 6). An ephah was a common measure of grain in antiquity. It is thought to approximate about five gallons (cf. Lev. 19:36; Ruth 2:17; 1 Sam. 1:24). Like our bushel, the term *ephah* was applied both to the measure and the container.

The interpreting angel then added a word of explanation, "This is their appearance in all the land." The words "their appearance" literally reads "their eye." But the Hebrew word *eye* has a broad range of meaning and may be translated "appearance" as in Leviticus 13:55 and Numbers 11:7. Many scholars, however, have argued for emending the text to read "their iniquity" instead of "their eye." This emendation, which is supported by the Septuagint and Syriac versions, involves merely the substitution of the Hebrew letter *waw* for the letter *yod*. It is argued that the sense of the text is greatly improved by this emendation.[24]

That proposed change would involve a smoothing of the text and is based on scanty evidence, because no Hebrew manuscript records this reading. The emendation does not really enhance the reader's understanding of the text, for the explanation provided in verse 8 ("This is Wickedness!") is quite sufficient. Although widely accepted, the proposed change from "eye" (i.e., "appearance") to "iniquity" is unnecessary and lacks merit. The antecedent of the possessive

23. T. T. Perowne, *Haggai and Zechariah* (Cambridge: At the University Press, 1886), p. 60.
24. Baldwin, *Haggai, Zechariah, Malachi,* p. 128.

pronoun "their" must be determined from the context and probably refers to the perpetrators of the wickedness (cf. 5:8).

In verse 7 Zechariah observes a lead cover on the ephah being lifted, and the interpreting angel calls his attention to a woman sitting or crouching inside the container. It has been observed that a normal-sized woman would be unable to fit in a five-gallon basket. That is of little real difficulty in apocalyptic literature noted for supernatural and unusual circumstances.

The significance of the woman in the ephah is revealed by the interpreting angel in verse 8: "This is wickedness!" The female figure depicted in the vision is the personification of sin. Baldwin notes that it is because the Hebrew word is feminine that "Wickedness" is personified as a woman.[25] Taken with verse 6 the woman in the ephah represents the wickedness of the people in the land. The woman apparently makes an attempt to escape from the ephah, is thrown down into the middle of it, and the lead weight is once again placed on the opening.

THE REMOVAL TO SHINAR (5:9-11)

Zechariah has seen the filthy garments being removed from Joshua (3:4); he now observes the woman in the ephah being removed from the land. The woman in the ephah is carried away by two women who "had wings like the wings of a stork." The stork is a familiar migratory bird frequently seen traveling north along the Jordan Valley in the spring of the year. The bird is noted for its broad and powerful wings and is capable of flying high ("between the earth and heavens") and for long distances. The simile "like the wings of a stork," and the additional comment that the two women came "with the wind in their wings," suggest that the ephah was removed swiftly and efficiently. There are no grounds for the view that the two women *assist* wickedness in her escape from destruction by carrying her to Babylon. There is no explanation pro-

25. Ibid., p. 129.

vided by the interpreting angel as to why the two agents are women. Apparently their gender is not significant for our understanding of the vision.

As Zechariah sees the ephah being lifted high into the sky, he asks the interpreting angel, "Where are they taking the ephah?" (5:10). He is told that the woman in the ephah is being removed to the land of Shinar to build a "temple" for her there (5:11). "Shinar" is an ancient name for the district in which the cities of Babylon (Babel), Erech, Accad (or Akkad), and Calneh were located (Gen. 10:10; 11:2). The prophets used the term to refer to Babylon (Isa. 11:11; Dan. 1:2). From the earliest times the people of this region were noted for being opposed to God's will and ways. It was there that the people said, "Come, let us build for ourselves a city, and a tower whose top will reach into heaven, and let us make for ourselves a name" (Gen. 11:4).

The woman in the ephah was to be removed to the land of Israel's recent captivity and set there in her proper place. The word "temple" (literally translated "house") may refer either to a dwelling place or a place of worship. Because it is unlikely that the two women, God's agents for removing wickedness, would establish a false worship center, it is best to regard the "house" as merely a dwelling. The word "pedestal" is better translated "place" or "abode." When the house is prepared, the woman in the ephah shall be set there in her place. Contrary to the renderings by the NASB ("temple" and "pedestal"), there is nothing in the text that indicates that the woman will be worshiped as a goddess or idol in Babylon.

Whereas the sixth vision reveals that the wicked will be purged from Israel, the seventh reveals that wickedness will be removed from the land of Israel. The message of this vision is similar to that of the fourth vision, in which God declared, "I will remove the iniquity of that land in one day" (3:9). Ezekiel must have had the same thoughts in mind when he spoke of Israel's cleansing from uncleanness and renewal to spiritual vitality (Ezek. 36:25-29). God's people Israel may be encouraged, for wickedness will be judged and removed. One day, yet future, Israel will be purified. The seventh vision offers hope and encouragement for those of the restoration period, but the ultimate realization of that future hope awaits Israel's acceptance of Jesus as their Messiah.

THE FOUR CHARIOTS (6:1-8)

The first and last visions of Zechariah both have to do with Israel's relation to the Gentile nations. The two visions are similar, yet significantly different. In the first vision, the horses patrol the earth and report peace. In the last, chariots patrol the earth and dispense judgment. There seems to be little basis for the view of some scholars that the first vision takes place in the evening as the horses come in from every quarter, and the last vision takes place at dawn as the horses (now hitched to chariots) are sent out again. Although the two visions appear to balance each other, introducing and concluding the series, they are too dissimilar in detail to suggest such a close correspondence.

THE VISION DESCRIBED (6:1-3)

As the prophet lifted up his eyes again he beheld "four chariots . . . coming forth from between two mountains" (6:1). In ancient times two-wheeled, horse-drawn wagons or chariots served as vehicles for transportation. Some were particularly adapted for warfare. These war chariots usually had a crew of two or three men—a driver, a warrior, and a defender who manipulated a shield to protect the others. The chariots seen by Zechariah were probably war chariots, for they were associated with the execution of judgment.

The two mountains between which the chariots came are often identified as Mount Zion and the Mount of Olives. But no such identification is made by the interpreting angel, and the mountains in the vicinity of Jerusalem are limestone, not "bronze." Much has been made over the fact that the mountains were "bronze" (6:1). This is said by some to represent divine judgment. Others suggest that because bronze was used for weapons, the bronze mountains represent the impregnable defenses of God's heavenly abode. No one really knows, since the meaning was not explained by the interpreting angel. The fact that the mountains are bronze rather than rock or dirt merely suggests a supernatural rather than a natural setting.

Zechariah also observes that each of the four chariots were drawn by a team of horses—the first chariot by red horses, the second by black horses, the third by white horses, and the fourth by a team of strong, dappled horses. "Dappled" suggests white spots on a dark background. The descriptive term "strong" indicates that the fourth team was particularly powerful and active.

Some commentators have sought to find symbolic significance in the colors, suggesting that they represent characteristics of the four great world powers—Babylon, Medo-Persia, Greece, and Rome. Such speculation is both dangerous and unnecessary. The colors may simply serve to distinguish the chariots that proceed to the various quarters of the earth (cf. 6:6).

The vision of the four chariots bears some resemblance to the vision of the four horsemen in Revelation 6:1-8. The interpreter should, however, exercise caution in making anything of this. It should be remembered that similarity is not the same as identity, and in this case the differences are greater than any observable similarities.

THE VISION EXPLAINED (6:4-8)

As in the previous visions, Zechariah needs to be told its interpretation. He asks the angel who was speaking with him, "What are these, my lord?" (6:4). The interpreting angel then reveals the symbolic significance of the horse-drawn chariots. He declares in verse 5, "These are the four spirits of heaven, going forth after standing before the Lord of all the earth."

It is debated whether *ruhoth,* the word translated "spirits" in the NASB and "winds" in the KJV,* actually refers to

*King James Version.

angelic beings or is simply a metaphor indicating swiftness and ease. Psalm 104:4 refers to the "winds" as God's messengers, and the writer of Hebrews specifically applies this verse to angels (Heb. 1:7). The fact that the "spirits" are personalized as "standing before the Lord of all the earth" supports the view that they are angelic beings and agents of God's judgment. Certainly angels, not winds, are said to "stand" before God (cf. Luke 1:19; Zech. 3:4). There may be a play on the word *ruhoth* in verse 5. As the "winds" travel over the face of the earth, so the four "spirits" of heaven will go forth throughout the land to accomplish their divine commission.

There is some difficulty in the description of the horse-drawn chariots going forth. The black horses go to the north, and the white ones "go forth after them, while the dappled ones go forth to the south country" (6:6). It seems at first glance that the black and white teams go north, the dappled go south, and the red team is held in reserve. It has been suggested, however, that there is a phrase missing from the Hebrew text at the beginning of verse 6. Because neither the red horse nor the east is mentioned, the "missing" clause could be, "The red horses went towards the east country."[26] The *Jerusalem Bible* and the *New English Bible* incorporate this emendation into the text. However, this additional clause represents a conjecture not founded on any manuscript evidence.

It has also been suggested that the words "after them" used of the white team should be translated "behind them," that is, "to the west," as in Joshua 8:2 ("behind"). But the use of the terms "north country" and "south country" in Zechariah and their absence in Joshua 8:2 would argue against this interpretation. It seems best to take the verse at face value. The black and white teams went to the north, and the dappled team went south. The red team is not mentioned, and hence no direction is revealed. Whereas the red team may have

26. Ibid., p. 131.

waited in reserve as H. C. Leupold suggests,[27] the reference in verse 5 to the *four* spirits of heaven going forth indicates that they all went on patrol (cf. 6:7). The destination of the red team is simply not revealed.

The horses were apparently pulling at their harnesses, "eager to go" forth and patrol the earth (6:7). The adjective "strong" probably applies to all the horses, although it was used only of the dappled team in verse 3. They are issued the command "Go, patrol the earth," and they proceed on their mission. The One who issued the command is not identified. But the fact that the patrols are said in verse 8 to have "appeased My wrath" suggests that the commander is Yahweh. The horses are sent to patrol the whole earth for the "Lord of all the earth" (cf. 6:5).

The Commander of the chariot teams then addresses Zechariah directly, calling attention to what His agents have accomplished. "See, those who are going to the land of the north have appeased My wrath in the land of the north." The words "appeased My wrath" may be literally translated "caused My spirit to rest." God's spirit is at rest because His agents have executed His judgment. This judgment was accomplished in part by the anointed servant Cyrus as God gave him victory over Babylon in 539 B.C. (cf. Isa. 13:1-22; 45:1-5). Victory in the turbulent north—ever a threat against Israel—suggests that victory is achieved over every foe. Indeed, the chariot teams are assigned to patrol the "earth."

The eighth and final vision of Zechariah reveals that divine judgment will be executed on the Gentile nations. This judgment will give God's spirit rest by bringing just retribution on those who have persecuted His people Israel. God's spirit has yet to be at complete rest, for although Babylon has fallen, other Gentile nations have yet to be judged (cf. Joel 3:1-17; Matt. 25:31-46).

27. Leupold, *Exposition of Zechariah,* p. 117.

THE CROWNING OF JOSHUA (6:9-15)

The eight night visions of Zechariah are followed by the symbolic crowning of Joshua the high priest. This symbolic act and the message that accompanies it brings into sharp focus the messianic implications of the prophetic visions. While distinct in its literary form, the symbolic crowning of Joshua is linked thematically to the preceding visions and forms a fitting climax to this section.

THE SYMBOLIC ACTION (6:9-11)

Instead of seeing a mysterious vision that must be explained by an interpreting angel, Zechariah now is among the people and receives a command from the Lord. The introductory formula "The word of the LORD also came to me saying" (6:9; cf. 4:8; 7:4; 8:1, 18) indicates that a message, rather than a vision, is to be received.

Zechariah is commanded by the Lord to take (or "receive") an "offering" from Heldai, Tobijah, and Jedaiah, three recent arrivals in Jerusalem from Babylon. Although there were three major returns from captivity—the first under Sheshbazzar in 537 B.C., the second under Ezra in 458 B.C., and the third under Nehemiah in 444 B.C.—apparently there were other smaller groups of Jews who trickled back to the land. The group mentioned here came with a gift for the needy restoration community. The word "offering" is not actually in the Hebrew text but is implied from the context (cf. 6:11). Zechariah is told to enter the house of Josiah the son of Zephaniah, where the recent arrivals from Babylon were lodged (6:10).

In the house of Josiah, Zechariah is to take silver and gold from the offering of the exiles and fashion a crown that is to be placed on the head of Joshua the high priest (6:11). "Crown" is actually a plural word and has been variously interpreted. It has been suggested that the "crown" was a composite of a number of circlets that could be worn singly or fitted together (cf. Rev. 19:12). That view is supported by the reference to the two precious metals—"silver and gold." Others have viewed the plural as a superlative denoting excellence or majesty as in the designation *Elohim* (God), the plural of *El*. It has also been argued that the word *crown* bears an archaic ending (*ot*), which suggests that the crown belongs to the sacred realm. The various explanations may not be mutually exclusive. The crown was probably ornate, made up of several circlets, and had commemorative significance.

Zechariah is instructed to place the crown on the "head of Joshua the son of Jehozadak, the high priest." It has been argued by some commentators that Zechariah expected the messianic prophecies to be fulfilled in Zerubbabel (cf. 4:7, 9), and hence "Zerubbabel" rather than "Joshua" was the original name in verse 11.[28] However, Zechariah 4:7, 9 can be satisfactorily interpreted as referring to the Zerubbabel of the restoration period without messianic significance. Second, no Hebrew text or ancient version suggests that "Zerubbabel" was the original reading. Most significant, the absence of the article in verse 12 ("Behold a man") indicates that "someone other than either Joshua or Zerubbabel is meant."[29] Similarly, the view that both Joshua and Zerubbabel were crowned has little to commend it. Such hypotheses are based on conjecture and a naturalistic rewriting of Restoration History.

THE MESSIANIC SIGNIFICANCE (6:12-15)

Verses 12-15 record a divine message that Zechariah is commanded to deliver to Joshua the high priest. This message explains the messianic significance of the crowning of Joshua. The first part of the message reveals God's plan for the building of a future Temple for His people. Yahweh of hosts declares, "Behold, a man whose name is Branch, for He will

---

branch out from where He is; and He will build the temple of the LORD" (6:12) It has already been noted that the absence of the definite article ("a man") draws attention to the fact that someone other than either Joshua or Zerubbabel is meant. That one is identified as "Branch," a messianic term used by the prophets in referring to both royal and priestly functions (cf. Isa. 4:2; Jer. 23:3-5; 33:14-26; Zech. 3:8).[30]

It is said that the Branch "will branch out from where He is." That is, he will be what his name implies—one who shoots up and branches out as a strong, vigorous plant. Although He comes from parched ground where there is little chance of his succeeding (Isa. 53:2), nevertheless He will prosper. Indeed, "He will build the temple of the LORD." This thought is repeated in verse 13 for emphasis. In view of the fact that the restoration Temple was already being built and would be completed by Zerubbabel (cf. 4:9), the Temple referred to here must be the future Temple of the messianic kingdom (cf. Isa. 2:2-4; Ezek. 40-42; Mic. 4:1-5; Hag. 2:7-9).

Not only will Messiah the Branch build the millennial Temple, He "will bear the honor and sit and rule on His throne" (6:13). The word *honor* is used often in the Old Testament to signify the majesty or splendor of the king (Jer. 22:18) and of God (Ps. 96:6). The Branch will enjoy royal splendor and majesty as He exercises authority from His throne. The "throne" is that royal throne promised David's house forever (2 Sam. 7:12-16). The office of king would never pass from David's line. Gabriel's words to Mary reveal that Jesus is the One who will occupy that throne and rule the people of Israel in a kingdom that will have no end (Luke 1:32-33).

The words in verse 13, "Thus, He will be a priest on His throne," have troubled many commentators. Because it is unlikely that a priest would be "on" a throne, many have appealed to the Septuagint and translated "at his right hand." The phrase is interpreted to mean that the priest (Joshua) would enjoy power and honor second only to the king (Zerub-

30. Ibid., pp. 93-97.

babel). Mastin argues convincingly that it is not legitimate to appeal to the Septuagint as evidence for a different translation of the Hebrew text.[31] The usual meaning of the preposition in question is "upon" or "over," which makes the best sense in the context.

The Lord then declares, "The counsel of peace will be between the two offices [literally, 'between both of them']" (6:13). Whereas in the past there had been rivalries between Israel's civil and religious leadership, the union of king and priest in one person—the Branch—will bring about perfect harmony. Baldwin notes, "Nowhere else in the Old Testament is it made so plain that the coming Davidic king will also be a priest."[32] The king-priest theme is also developed in Psalm 110 and Hebrews 7.

In verse 14 Zechariah is told that the ornate crown that had been placed on the head of Joshua the high priest will "become a reminder in the temple of the LORD to Helem, Tobijah, Jedaiah, and Hen the son of Zephaniah." The crown was to be deposited in the Temple as a memorial to those Jews who had brought gifts to Jerusalem from Babylon. It would also have served as a reminder of the teaching concerning the union of king and priest in one Person, the coming Messiah.

The variation of the name Heldai/Helem (6:10, 14) may be attributed to the fact that the names of biblical characters often take more than one form as in Uzziah/Azariah, king of Judah (2 Kings 14:20; 2 Chron. 26:1). The name "Hen the son of Zephaniah" corresponds to the name "Josiah the son of Zephaniah" in verse 10. "Hen" may be a substitute for Josiah, but there is a good possibility that it served as a title. Aaron Demsky argues that the Hebrew word translated "Hen" (literally, "to Hen," *lhn*) is the equivalent of an Aramaic term for a temple or court steward. He traces the

31. B. A. Mastin, "A Note on Zechariah VI 13," *Vetus Testamentum* 26 (1976): 113-16.
32. Baldwin, *Haggai, Zechariah, Malachi,* p. 137.

linguistic derivation and presents a convincing case that Josiah was in charge of the cultic apparel in the Jerusalem Temple and that the reference to him in verse 14 uses his title "Temple Steward" rather than his personal name.[33]

The Lord adds in verse 15, "And those who are far off will come and build the temple of the LORD." The Temple referred to is not Zerubbabel's, which was almost complete, but the same one mentioned in verses 12 and 13—the millennial Temple. As Jews came from far off Babylon bringing offerings of silver and gold to Jerusalem, so those "who are far off" will contribute to the building of the Temple in the coming kingdom. Those "far off" include Gentiles (cf. 2:11; 8:22; Hag. 2:7-9; Eph. 2:13).

Zechariah affirms that the fulfillment of his prophecies will authenticate him as a messenger sent from God (cf. 2:9, 11; 4:9). He concludes with a warning, "And it will take place, if you completely obey the LORD your God." Those words are similar to those of Deuteronomy 28:1, where Israel is promised blessings for obedience. Although the fulfillment of the prophecy is certain, it is only through obedience that those promises will be realized personally.

The symbolic crowning of Joshua serves to illustrate the prophetic message of the coming of One who will fill both the offices of king and priest. With the gifts of both Jews and Gentiles, He will build the millennial Temple and exercise peaceful dominion on His throne. As Walter C. Kaiser comments, "Princely gifts coming from the far-off Babylon were but a harbinger and precursor of the wealth of the nations that would pour into Jerusalem when Messiah the Branch was received as King of kings and Lord of lords."[34]

---

33. Aaron Demsky, "The Temple Steward Josiah ben Zephaniah," *Israel Exploration Journal* 31 (1981): 100-102.
34. Walter C. Kaiser, *Toward an Old Testament Theology* (Grand Rapids: Zondervan, 1978), p. 254.

3

THE QUESTION
CONCERNING FASTING

(ZECHARIAH 7-8)

Chapters 7-8 deal with a matter that was of utmost concern for the Jews in Babylon—the observance of religious fasts. Fasting was a means of commemorating certain events that were significant on Israel's religious calendar. This section of Zechariah deals with the relative merit of such fasts and reveals that in view of what God has begun to do, the fasts of His people would become feasts. The core of this section is found in 7:1-7 and 8:18-19. There is no need, however, to regard the remainder of the text merely as an unrelated collection of sermon material and sayings. These chapters form a literary unit and contain a unified message.

THE INQUIRY BY THE MEN OF BETHEL (7:1-3)

The third major section of Zechariah begins with a date that distinguishes chronologically the sermon on fasting from the previous night visions. It was in the fourth year of the reign of King Darius (522-486 B.C.), or 518 B.C., that the word of Yahweh came again to Zechariah. It was the fourth day of Chislev, the Babylonian name for the ninth month that corresponds to December on the Julian calendar. According to Babylonian records, the new moon of the ninth month appeared on December 4, 518 B.C. The date of the prophecy may then be calculated as December 7, 518 B.C. More than two years had passed since the beginning of Zechariah's prophetic ministry (1:1) and the resumption of building activities at the Temple (Hag. 1:12-15). It had been fourteen months since

Zechariah had received his eight night visions (1:7). Verse 1 contains the last date given in Zechariah. The date probably applies only to the events and prophecies of chapters 7 and 8.

Verse 2 indicates that a delegation of Jews had been sent to Jerusalem "to seek the favor of the LORD." The expression "to seek the favor of" may be literally translated "to appease the face of" and suggests the presentation of offerings and worship (8:21, 22; Mal. 1:9). There is considerable debate as to *who* sent the delegation and *who* was sent.

It has been suggested that Darius (7:1) did the sending. This view, however, involves unnecessary alteration of the Hebrew text. The translations of the NASB and RSV* reflect the view that Jews from the city of Bethel, located twelve miles north of Jerusalem, sent the delegation. More than two hundred Jews from Bethel returned from Babylon in 537 B.C. (Ezra 2:28; Neh. 7:32), and the city was reoccupied during the restoration period (Neh. 11:3). This community of Jews may have sent a delegation to Jerusalem to worship and inquire regarding the necessity of continuing certain fasts.

A number of commentators hold the view that the delegation was sent by Jews yet in Babylon. It is argued that the word "Bethel" is part of a compound personal name, "Bethel-Sharezer," of which the Babylonian equivalent occurs in texts dating from around 540 B.C.[1] This view is attractive in that it accounts for the delay of three and a half months between the last fast (7:3) and their arrival (7:1). However, the view involves dropping the "and" between "Sharezer" and "Regemmelech." It is probably best to regard the delegation as having been sent by the Jewish community in the city of Bethel.

As to the matter of who was sent, it has been pointed out that "Regemmelech" does occur at Ugarit as the title of the king's spokesman.[2] That may suggest that the leader of the

*Revised Standard Version.

1. J. P. Hyatt, "A Neo-Babylonian Parallel to BETHEL-SAR-EZER, Zech. 7, 2," *Journal of Biblical Literature* 56 (1937): 387-94.
2. Joyce Baldwin, *Haggai, Zechariah, Malachi,* p. 142.

delegation had royal authority. But such royal authority was
absent in Bethel. The suggestion that the delegation was sent
by Jewish leaders in Babylon under Persian governmental
authority has merit but seems to involve many assumptions.
It is suggested here that the delegation was made up of Jews
sent by the religious leaders of Bethel and included Sharezer
and Regemmelech and "their men," apparently some subor-
dinates or assistants.

The question put to the priests and prophets at Jerusalem
concerned the necessity of continuing periodic seasons of
humiliation to commemorate such events as the 586 B.C.
destruction of the Jerusalem Temple. These seasons of
humiliation (cf. Ezra 10:6) involved shedding tears ("Shall I
weep") and fasting ("and abstain"). The particular season
mentioned was in the "fifth" month—the month that the
Temple was destroyed (2 Kings 25:8). Other fasts mentioned
in 8:19 commemorated the breaching of the city walls in the
fourth month (Jer. 39:2), the slaying of Gedaliah in the
seventh month (2 Kings 25:25), and the beginning of
Nebuchadnezzar's siege in the tenth month (2 Kings 25:1-2).
Those fasts continued throughout the Babylonian captivity.
In view of the return to the land and resumption of the
Temple-building, were fasts that commemorated the past
destruction of the Jewish state appropriate?

THE LORD'S REBUKE OF EMPTY RITUALISM (7:4-7)

The question concerning the continuation of certain fasts is
not answered directly. Apparently it was first necessary to
deal with the attitudes and motives of the people. God is not
so much concerned with the outward activity as with the in-
ward attitude that motivates it.

The word of the Lord came to Zechariah (7:5), and he was
instructed to address both the Jewish people and the priests.
God used two rhetorical questions to probe the hearts of the
hearers. "When you fasted and mourned in the fifth and
seventh months these seventy years, was it actually for Me
that you fasted?" (v. 5). The fast in the fifth month com-

memorated the destruction of the Temple (2 Kings 25:8), and that of the seventh month commemorated the assassination of Gedaliah, the Jewish governor appointed by Nebuchadnezzar (2 Kings 25:25; Jer. 41:1-3). The "seventy" years of captivity may be calculated either from the first deportation (605 B.C.) to the beginning of the Temple rebuilding (536 B.C.) or from the destruction of the Temple (586 B.C.)to the completion of the rebuilt Temple (515 B.C.)[3] The latter view is preferred because it best coincides with the fasts mentioned in the verse (cf. 1:12).

The Lord's rhetorical question implies that the fasting was motivated by selfish concern rather than to honor Him. Verse 6 completes the thought, "And when you eat and drink, do you not eat for yourselves and do you not drink for yourselves?" As their daily eating and drinking was motivated by a natural desire to meet personal needs, so was their fasting. The fasts were no different from the observance of regular meals, in view of the self-centeredness of the people. Zechariah acknowledges that religious ritual observed for selfish reasons does not qualify as true worship (cf. John 4:23-24). God's perspective on fasting is set forth in Isaiah 58:3-7. Hand ritual apart from heart righteousness finds no favor with God.

Verse 7 contains the words of the prophet. He points out that the teachings of verses 5 and 6 are nothing new. Indeed Yahweh proclaimed them by the former (i.e., "earlier") prophets in the period before the Exile (cf. 2 Chron. 36:15-16). Zechariah may even have reference to Isaiah's instructions regarding fasting (Isa. 58:3-7). Zechariah's prophecies were in continuity with those messengers of God who preceded him. The "Negev" refers to the dry southland of Judah centering on Beersheba (Josh. 15:21-32). The "foothills" (literally *shephelah*), or "lowlands," refers to the transitional region between the hill country of Judah and the coastal plain (cf. Josh. 15:33-47).

---

3. J. Carl Laney, *Ezra-Nehemiah*, p. 129.

THE LORD'S REQUIREMENT OF PRACTICAL RIGHTEOUSNESS (7:8-14)

The Lord has little interest in empty ritual, but He delights in the practical righteousness that results from obeying His Word. The rest of chapter 8 focuses on the requirements of true religion that were set forth by the earlier prophets and disregarded by the generation that went into exile. The introductory formula in verse 8 does not necessarily indicate a break or time lapse between this and the previous section. By appealing to Yahweh, Zechariah introduces a new topic and affirms once again that his message originates with God. In verses 9 and 10 the Lord brings four precepts to the attention of the people. These practical precepts reflect the burden of the prophets in the area of social concern (cf. Isa. 1:11-17; Hos. 6:6; Mic. 6:6-8, see also James 1:27).

The first precept, "Dispense true justice," reflects God's concern for truth. Judicial decision must be made without partiality, or bias. Such is the concern of the righteous man (Ezek. 18:8). The second precept, "Practice kindness and compassion each to his brother, " speaks more to the area of day to day dealings with others. The word *kindness* may be translated "loyal love" and suggests a covenant-like commitment to others (cf. Gen. 20:13; 2 Sam. 16:17). The word *compassion* is related to the word for "womb" and suggests a mother's sense of love and concern. The third precept forbids the oppression of the widow, the orphan, the stranger, or the poor (7:10a). God's concern for the helpless and less fortunate (Ex. 22:21-24) is repeatedly emphasized by the prophets (Isa. 1:17, 23; Jer. 7:6; 22:3; 49:11; Ezek. 22:7). The fourth precept forbids the devising of evil against one another (7:10b). This precept is repeated in 8:17. Fasting without obeying such foundational precepts constitutes religious hypocrisy and is repugnant to God (1 Sam. 15:22; Ps. 40:6-8).

Verse 11 tells of the response of the people to the earlier prophets—those who ministered before the Exile. "But they refused to pay attention, and turned a stubborn shoulder and stopped their ears from hearing." Like a stubborn animal that refuses to allow a yoke upon its neck (cf. Neh. 9:29; Hos.

4:16), the people of Israel refused to submit to God's ways. The third phrase brings the matter to a climax. The people plugged their ears against God's Word (cf. Isa. 6:10). Rather than allowing the words of the prophets to penetrate their hearts, the people "made their hearts like flint" so they could not hear the instruction Yahweh was providing by His Spirit (7:12). "Flint," or "emery," suggests the hardest of substances and could possibly be translated "diamond" (cf. Jer. 17:1; Ezek. 3:9). So hard were the hearts of the people that they could not hear the prophets' exhortations from the Torah or their revelations sent by God's Spirit (cf. Neh. 9:30; 2 Pet. 1:20-21).

The refusal of Israel to obey resulted in the execution of God's judgment. "Therefore great wrath came from the LORD of hosts." The judgment of God on His disobedient people should have been no surprise. Such discipline had been promised when the covenant was enacted (cf. Lev. 26:14-43; Deut. 28:15-68). The destruction of Jerusalem and exile to Babylon was the culmination of that divine discipline (2 Chron. 36:15-17).

Verses 13 and 14 elaborate on the thought of God's wrath mentioned in verse 12. Verse 13 indicates that the judgment was retribution according to kind. As the people had refused to listen to God's Word, so He would not listen when they called upon Him (cf. Jer. 11:11). The change in person from "He" to "I" is not uncommon in the prophets and reflects the vividness of the message in the mind of Zechariah.[4]

Verse 14 reveals the tragic consequences of Israel's disobedience. As by a mighty storm wind, they were whirled into exile among the foreign nations (Deut. 28:63-64). During the Babylonian captivity the Jewish people were strangers in a foreign land, and their own land was left desolate behind them. The extent of the desolation is suggested by the words "so that no one went back and forth." The "pleasant" land that was so much a part of the covenant between God and His

4. Baldwin, *Haggai, Zechariah, Malachi*, p. 148.

people (Gen. 12:1; 13:14-17; 15:18; Josh. 1:3-6; cf. Deut. 30:1-10) was desolate and forsaken. The description of the land as "flowing with milk and honey" (Ex. 3:8) does not reflect conditions in Israel during the Exile.

The Lord desires the worship of His people (John 4:23), but that worship must reflect spiritual realities. Sacrifices, offerings, and fasts are of little interest to God if accompanied by disobedience and hypocrisy. The record of God's dealing with the former generation undoubtedly gave the inquirers from Bethel cause to reflect on the motivation and conduct of their countrymen.

THE FUTURE RESTORATION OF ZION (8:1-17)

Whereas Zechariah 7:8-14 looks back to the past and focuses on God's discipline for disobedience, the next section looks to the future and focuses on the coming peace and prosperity of Zion. In the past the people neglected the requirements of the law and were punished. Now messianic promises are set forth to encourage the people in their ethical responsibilities (8:14-17). The prophet turns from the subject of Judah's past desolation to speak of her future restoration.

Some commentators have divided chapter 8 into ten units based on the "ten" occurrences of the formula "Thus says the LORD of hosts" (8:2, 3, 4, 6, 7, 9, 14, 20, 23). But the formula in verse 3 lacks the words "of hosts," and that casts some doubt on the ten-unit scheme. The two introductory statements, "Then the word of the LORD of hosts came to me ["to me" in 8:18 only] saying," (8:1, 18) appear to provide the key to the structure of the chapter. Accordingly, chapter 8 may be divided into two main sections (8:17; 8:18-23).

THE PROMISE OF RESTORATION (8:1-8)

The promise of Jerusalem's restoration clearly refers to the future, for the events recorded here have not yet happened. Following the introductory formula (8:1), Zechariah declares Yawheh's great love for His people. "Thus says the LORD of hosts, 'I am exceedingly jealous for Zion, yes, with great wrath I am jealous for her' " (8:3). The jealousy of God for His people, first spoken of at the giving of the law at Sinai (Ex. 20:5), is a measure of the intensity of His love. So great is God's love that He tolerates no rivals (Ex. 34:14) and elicits "great wrath" upon those who would oppose His people (cf., 1:14-15).

In verse 3 the Lord promises His presence among His people: "I will return to Zion and will dwell in the midst of Jerusalem." The Lord's presence among His people is the key to the blessings that follow (cf. 8:3b-6). The promise expands on thoughts introduced in 1:16-17 and 2:10 and anticipates the messianic era. In that future day Jerusalem will be called "the City of Truth," and the Temple mount will be recognized as "the Holy Mountain." The word translated "truth" may suggest more the idea of faithfulness or reliability, hence "the faithful city" (cf. Isa. 1:21, 26). The Temple mount will be recognized as "holy" because the Lord's presence will sanctify it as a place of true worship.

In verses 4 and 5 Zechariah anticipates that in the future messianic era, Jerusalem will be inhabited and secure. Jerusalem will be occupied by "old men" and "old women," whose longevity will testify not only to the absence of war and famine but also to the favor and blessing of the Lord (cf. Ex. 20:12; Isa. 65:20). The imagery of boys and girls playing in the "streets" or "squares" (literally "broad places") suggests a time of prosperity and security. It is a picture of divine blessing. These words would have been of special encouragement for the Jews of the restoration community, for at the time Zechariah ministered, the city of Jerusalem was only sparsely populated (cf. Neh. 7:4; 11:1-2).

The words of verse 6 are given for those who might lack the faith to believe God for such a glorious future. "If it is too difficult in the sight of the remnant of this people in those days, will it also be too difficult in My sight?" The rhetorical question implies that nothing is too difficult for God (Gen. 18:14; Matt. 19:26; Luke 1:37). The wonderful events just described are not beyond God's power. The words "in those days" indicate that the prophet is speaking of a future era.

In Verses 7 and 8 the Lord announces a future regathering of His people to Jerusalem. Undoubtedly many of the returned exiles were discouraged by the fact that so few Jews had returned to their homeland. The vast majority remained in Babylon, apparently "not willing to leave their possessions" (Josephus, *Antiquities* XI.8). Yet, in the future things would be different. The Lord would "save," or "deliver," His people from captivity a second time (Isa. 11:11). The terms "east' and "west" serve to represent all parts of the earth (cf. Matt. 24:31). As anticipated in Deuteronomy 30:1-6, God will not only bring His people back to their land but will restore them to their covenant relationship with Himself. Yahweh declares, "And they will be My people and I will be their God in truth and righteousness" (v. 8).

The covenant relationship between God and His people (Ex. 19:5; 29:45; Lev. 26:12) had been adulterated by Israel's persistent disobedience (Hos. 1:2-9). But Zechariah anticipates a renewal of God's covenant with His people (cf. Deut. 30:6; Jer. 31:33; Ezek. 36:28; Hos. 2:23). In that happy day "truth" (or "faithfulness" and "righteousness") will characterize the relationship between Israel and their God. Whereas God has always displayed those attributes in His dealings with His people, in the future His faithfulness and righteous dealings toward Israel will be reciprocated.

THE ENCOURAGEMENT FOR THE PRESENT (8:9-13)

Having set forth the prospect of Israel's future restoration, the Lord encourages the remnant of the returned exiles in their present struggle. Verse 9 contains essentially the same message as Haggai 2:4 by exhorting the people to "be strong" and persevere in the rebuilding of the Temple. The words "Let your hands be strong" are used as an expression for the strength and courage necessary for battle (cf. Judg. 7:11; 2 Sam. 2:7; 16:21). The exhortation is addressed to "you who are listening in these days to these words from the mouths of the prophets.'' Those words identify the intended recipients of this message with Zechariah's contemporaries.

The "prophets" (v. 9) were those who spoke in the day that the repairs began on the Temple. No prophets are mentioned in Ezra 3 in connection with setting up the altar and laying the Temple foundation in 536 B.C. It is tempting to identify "the prophets" with Haggai and Zechariah, but their first recorded prophecies are dated in the year 520 B.C. (Hag. 1:1; Zech. 1:1). They encouraged the *completion* of the Temple building some sixteen years after the foundation had been laid (Ezra 5:1-2). Verse 9 may be an indication that Haggai and Zechariah also ministered at the founding of the Temple. Otherwise the "prophets" mentioned here are unknown.

Verse 10 recounts the desperate situation in Judea before the work on the Temple resumed in 520 B.C. (cf. Hag. 1:16, 10-11; 2:16-17). Those days were characterized by scarcity ("no wage") both for man and beast. Hostility ("no peace") characterized the relationship between the Judeans and their foreign neighbors—the Samaritans and the surrounding nations (Ezra 4:1-5; 5:3; 6:6, 13). In addition to the divine discipline of scarcity and hostility, the Lord "set all men one against another." Disunity and strife characterized the interpersonal relationships of the returned exiles. Scarcity, hostility, and disunity were all evidences of God's discipline on His forgetful people (cf. Deut. 28:38-40, 49-52, 54-56).

In verse 11 the key words "But now" indicate that a new state of things has come about. Whereas in the past the people had been subject to God's discipline for their disobedience, now in view of their obedience they will enjoy His blessing (Hag. 2:18-19).

As verse 10 reflects the cursings of the covenant (Lev. 26:14-33; Deut. 28:15-68), verse 12 reflects the blessings of the covenant (Lev. 26:1-13; Deut. 28:1-14) that the obedient may anticipate. The expression "peace for the seed" refers to a time of peace for the sowing of the seed. As a result the men can focus on planting their fields rather than defending their land. Thus the vine will bear its fruit, and the land will yield its produce. God also promises that the heavens will give their dew—moisture that is vital to the growing of crops in a land with virtually no rainfall during the summer months (cf. Hag. 1:10). God promsies all those blessings to the faithful remnant of His people.

Verse 13 provides a summary of the main thoughts of this section, contrasting Israel's past and future. In the past, disobedient Israel served as a prime example of a people experiencing God's judgment. But in the future they will be a people known for divine blessing. In fulfillment of God's promise to Abraham (Gen. 12:3), Israel will become a blessing to the nations. God's words "I will save you" make all the difference. God's intervention in behalf of His own, delivering them both physically and spiritually, will bring about the blessing promised here. Note that Zechariah anticipates the inclusion of both Judah and Israel in the future deliverance and blessing (cf. Jer. 31:31-34; Ezek. 37:15-28).

The Lord concludes His words of encouragement for the present struggle with the exhortation "Do not fear; let your hands be strong." In view of God's gracious purposes and future plans for His people, they are called to be diligent in their present efforts, trusting the outcome to God.

THE OBLIGATIONS OF OBEDIENCE (8:14-17)

Having informed His people of His plans to bless them, the Lord reveals the obligations that His love and grace entail. Verses 14 and 15 contrast God's past and present purposes with regard to His people. In the past He "purposed to do harm" to them in view of their disobedience. The tragedies that befell Judah were not circumstantial. They were in accordance with God's purposive planning (cf. Jer. 4:28; 51:12). The words "And I have not relented" may be better translated "And I did not repent." They reveal the unchangeableness of God's purposes in spite of the severe discipline required by His people. He is not like a man that He should change His mind (1 Sam. 15:29).

In view of the people's response to the prophets (Hag. 1:12-14), the Lord has purposed "to do good to Jerusalem and the house of Judah." With the work on the Temple resumed, a new era of prosperity could begin (8:12-13). "Jerusalem and the house of Judah" comprehend the nation as a whole. The exhortation "Do not fear!" repeats the thought of verse 13. There is no need to fear that the promise will not be fulfilled. God's word is reliable.

But grace is not license to sin (Rom. 6:1). Obedience is the measure of one's genuine love for God (John 14:15). Having highlighted His gracious plans for His people, the Lord sets forth in verses 16 and 17 the ethical obligations they incur by virtue of their special relationship with Him. As in 7:9-10, the Lord declares both positively and negatively what the people should do.

Verse 16 contains the two positive injunctions. Both focus on the high priority of truth in dealing with others. Truth is both an attribute of God (Ex. 34:6) and a subject of His concern (Ps. 15:2; Hos. 4:1-2). The words "speak the truth" are quoted by Paul in Ephesians 4:25. The command, "Judge with truth and judgment for peace in your gates," reflects God's concern for truth in judicial decisions. The "gates" of ancient cities served as meeting places for the elders when deciding disputes (cf. Deut. 21:19; Ruth 4:1-12). The judgments passed are to be in accordance with the truth and make for peace and harmony among those involved.

Verse 17 contains two negative injunctions. God forbids the planning of evil against others and condemns the love for false oaths. Bearing false testimony is specifically forbidden in the Decalogue (Ex. 20:16; cf. 23:1). Perjury, or the use of falsified evidence, seems to have been a serious problem among the returned exiles (cf. 5:4). The Lord declares in no uncertain terms that such evil plans and falsehoods are utterly repugnant to Him, "For all these are what I hate." These sins are listed among the seven "abominations" enumerated in Proverbs 6:16-19.

THE FUTURE JOYS OF GOD'S PEOPLE (8:18-23)

The second major section of chapter 8 describes the future joys of God's people as they worship God and fulfill their destiny to be a light and a blessing to the nations.

FASTS WILL BECOME FEASTS (8:18-19)

At last the answer to the men from Bethel is given. They had inquired regarding the appropriateness of continuing periodic seasons of fasting to commemorate events associated with the 586 B.C. destruction of Jerusalem and the Temple (7:1-3). Having dealt with the matter of empty ritual, which reflects little practical righteousness, and promised restoration of blessing to obedient Zion, the Lord now declares that the fasts of the past will be replaced with feasts. In view of what God has been doing among His people, the mourning is over. A new era has dawned.

The four fasts mentioned here commemorated the breaching of the city walls (Jer. 39:2); the destruction of the Temple (2 Kings 25:8); the slaying of Gedaliah (2 Kings 25:25; and the beginning of Nebuchadnezzar's siege (2 Kings 25:1, 2). Those seasons of fasting will become "joy, gladness, and cheerful feasts for the house of Judah." They will be "cheerful" in that they will commemorate the good things God is doing among His people. Isaiah anticipates a similar reversal of circumstances in connection with Messiah's future work for Israel (Isa., 61:2-3), Such mercies from the Lord should stimulate a willingness to obey His commands. Hence, the Lord adds the ethical injunction, "So love truth and peace" (cf. 8:16).

FOREIGNERS WILL SEEK GOD (8:20-23)

The Lord goes on to announce a great turning of the nations to God. Similar thoughts are expressed in Isaiah 2:2-4 and Micah 4:1-5 concerning the future messianic era. In the third vision the prophet learned that a day would come when other nations would commit themselves to Yahweh and become His people (2:11). Now that turning to the Lord by the nations is elaborated. A great multitude of people from "many cities" will say to one another, "Let us go at once to entreat the favor of the LORD, and to seek the LORD of hosts" (8:21). Verses 20 and 21 emphasize the great number of people responding ("many") and the urgency they sense ("at once"). The expression "to entreat the favor of the LORD" reflects their desire to worship and offer sacrifices (cf. 7:2; Mal. 1:9). The words "I will also go" appear to be the reply of the one addressed. The response is positive.

Verse 22 records the result of this evangelistic work. "So many peoples and mighty nations will come to seek the LORD of hosts in Jerusalem and entreat the favor of the LORD." Three points are significant. First, the worshipers will include the peoples of many nations (i.e., Gentiles), not just Jews. Gentiles will be included among the people of God by faith (cf. Eph. 2:13-15, 17-19). Second, the worship will take place in Jerusalem. This is in keeping with other prophecies that identify Jerusalem as the center of worship during the messianic kingdom (14:16; Isa. 2:3; 66:20; Mic. 4:1-2). Third, the worship will involve Temple ritual and sacrifice. This is indicated by the expression "to entreat the favor of the LORD" (7:2; Mal. 1:9). The prophet Ezekiel describes this future Temple and its sacrificial ritual (Ezek. 40-44).

In that future day of spiritual renewal, the Jewish people will serve both as a light and a blessing to the nations (8:23), The Lord announces that the people of the foreign nations will grasp the garment of a Jew saying, "Let us go with you, for we have heard that God is with you." The fact that they "grasp the garment" suggests the intensity of their desire and their eagerness to appropriate Israel's faith. Although they are Gentiles by birth, those from the foreign nations may become the spiritual descendants of Abraham by personal faith (cf. Rom. 4:16; Gal. 3:7). As those who share Abraham's faith, they are one with the people of God and enjoy the spiritual blessings promised Abraham (Gen. 12:1-3; Jer. 31:31-34; Gal. 3:14). Quite clearly, the New or "Renewed" Covenant includes believing Gentiles (Ezek. 36:23-27; 2 Cor. 3:6; Heb. 8:6-13). It is an exciting prospect to think of Israel as a believing nation fulfilling her destiny as a light and a blessing to the nations (Gen. 12:3; Isa. 42:6; 49:6; 60:3).

4

THE ORACLE CONCERNING ISRAEL AND THE NATIONS

(ZECHARIAH 9-11)

The last six chapters of Zechariah deal primarily with Israel's eschatological future. Here the prophet details the prophetic program of Israel and the nations, especially in relation to the person and work of the coming Messiah. Zechariah 9-14 has a distinctive Christological emphasis, focusing particularly on the rejection and death of Christ. These chapters have been recognized as "the most quoted section of the prophets in the passion narratives of the Gospels."[1]

In terms of literary structure, Zechariah 9-14 contains two oracles, or "burdens" (9:1; 12:1). The first (9:1—11:17) records the rejection of the Messiah "Shepherd" (11:4-14). The second (12:1—14:21) records the ultimate acceptance of Messiah by the Jewish people and their spiritual cleansing (12:10—13:1).

THE DIVINE WARRIOR HYMN (9:1-17)

Chapter 9 records Yahweh's conflict with and victory over the foreign nations that He might establish His sovereignty and manifest His universal reign. Commentators have engaged in a great deal of discussion regarding the historical setting of the passage based on the allusions in the military campaign (9:1-7) and the reference to the sons of Greece (9:13). Scholars have argued for a historical setting during the reign

1. Joyce Baldwin, *Haggai, Zechariah, Malachi*, p. 59.

of Hezekiah, Josiah, Tiglath-pilneser, Sargon, Alexander, or the Maccabees. Most conservative commentators have followed the view that verses 1-7 predict the conquest of Alexander the Great because it fits well with the conservative view regarding the date of the book. The difficulty is that no one historical setting really answers the situation described in the passage. The text must be forced to serve one historical hypothesis or another.

Recently an alternative approach has been suggested. It has been argued that the literary genre of Zechariah 9 has been perceived incorrectly, and thus an inappropriate "historicizing method" of interpretation has been applied.[2] Instead of answering to a specific historical situation, Zechariah 9 appears to describe a cosmic war and reflect a particular genre of literature found in the ancient Near East. This literary form, found in such texts an Enuma Elish, the Ugaritic Baal Cycle, and Isaiah 52:7-12 has been designated a "Divine Warrior Hymn." At the heart of such a poem is the reenactment of the warrior-god's battle against the enemy, resulting in the reestablishment of peace. Paul D. Hanson further explains:

> The dominate tone of the composition is hymnic, being a celebration of the anticipated future act of Yahweh the Warrior. The function of the eschatological hymn in the apocalyptic literature is, however, a specialized one: the hymn, besides being a paean of praise, serves as an announcement of restoration to the faithful, thereby becoming a source of comfort in times of frustrated hopes and oppression.[3]

The approach suggested by Hanson has merit. First, this approach recognizes what others ignore, that a distinctive form of ancient Near Eastern literature appears in Zechariah 9. Second, it avoids the numerous hypotheses and endless debates over which historical situation is allegedly being

2. Paul D. Hanson, "Zechariah 9 and the Recapitulation of an Ancient Ritual Pattern," *Journal of Biblical Literature* 92 (March 1973): 37-59.
3. Ibid., p. 38 n. 2.

described. Third, the approach focuses on the general meaning of the text rather than speculating about particular
historical details. Baldwin takes a similar approach without
developing the literary genre of the passage:

> The writer is not taking any particular historical but . . . is us-
> ing past events to typify a supremely important future event.
> Just as successive alien armies swept through Syria and
> Palestine and claimed a right to each territory, so finally the
> Lord will see every proud city capitulate to Him.[4]

In the following comments, Zechariah 9 is viewed as a
"Divine Warrior Hymn" that prophetically depicts God's intervention among the nations with a view to the establishment
of the ideal kingdom that Yahweh has promised Israel as its
inheritance.

THE CONFLICT AND VICTORY (9:1-8)

Verse 1 identifies the prophecy as "the burden of the word
of the LORD." The word "burden" is used in an ominous
sense—a weighty judgment imposed on the prophet that he
must declare. The list of cities that follow have been connected with the campaigns of ancient rulers from Sargon to
the Maccabees. But trying to identify the particular campaign
involved has been an exercise in futility. Virtually all ancient
conquerers interested in controlling the eastern Mediterranean region followed basically the same route as they moved
from north to south. The hymn makes no mention of a
human conqueror. Rather it describes the march of a Divine
Warrior (cf. Ex. 15:2) who intervenes directly, apart from
human agents. It is best to view this city list as reflecting the
future subjugation of all the territories surrounding Israel
under Yahweh's authority (cf. 14:9).

The first part of verse 1 has no verb and could be translated, "The burden of the word of the LORD in Hadrach, with

---

4. Baldwin, *Haggai, Zechariah, Malachi*, p. 158.

Damascus as its resting place." The point is that the judgment
of Yahweh's prophetic word will be executed first in Hadrach
and then in Damascus. Hadrach ("Hatarika" in Assyrian in-
scriptions) is the northernmost of the places mentioned, being
situated north of Hamath on the Orontes River southwest of
Aleppo.[5] Damascus was the capital of Aram; the powerful
Arameans were long-standing enemies of Israel.

The rest of the verse appears to be explanatory ("for"), but
its meaning is debated. Some emend the text to read "cities of
Aram" instead of "eye of men." Others translate, "For
Yahweh has His eye on all mankind as on the tribes of
Israel." Although it is true that God providentially rules over
all the earth, the Masoretic pointing of the Hebrew word for
"eye" as a construct and the absence of a preposition ("on")
are difficult to explain.[6] Michell Dahood translates, "For the
LORD's is the surface of the earth, as well as all the tribes of
Israel."[7] A literal translation of the text would read, "For the
eye of man and of all the tribes of Israel (is) toward
Yahweh." It is possible that the preposition translated "for"
denotes result as in 1 Samuel 2:25. In that case, the thought
would be that all mankind, including Israel, is focusing attention on Yahweh as a result of the execution of His judgment
on Hadrach and Damascus.

Verse 2 reveals that Hamath also, which borders on
Damascus, will be the resting place of this prophetic judgment. Hamath is named in some texts as one of the northern
limits of the Promised Land (Num. 13:21; Josh. 13:5). Tyre
and Sidon on the Phoenician coast are also named as places
where the "burden" of Yahweh will rest. The worldly
wisdom of Tyre is acknowledged in Ezekiel 28:3-5. Judgment
will come on Tyre and Sidon despite their reputed wisdom.
Verse 3 reports that Tyre, in her worldly wisdom, has built

5. Merrill F. Unger, *Israel and the Aramaeans of Damascus* (London:
   James Clarke, 1957), p. 166 n. 12.
6. Charles L. Feinberg, *God Remembers,* p. 121.
7. Michell Dahood, "Zechariah 9:1," *Catholic Biblical Quarterly* (April
   1963): 123-24.

herself strong defenses to resist siege. She has acquired vast wealth through prosperous commerce (Ezek. 27:12-25) as security against economic woes. Yet those defenses would be to no avail (cf. Ps. 33:16-17). The Lord will dispossess (i.e., "impoverish") her and "cast her wealth into the sea" (9:4). What remains after this fatal blow to the economy of Tyre will be "consumed with fire." The complete overthrow of Tyre by Alexander the Great in 332 B.C. illustrates how even such a powerful city can be broken. Such are God's designs for those nations that resist His will.

Verses 5-7 describe the future judgment of God falling upon the chief cities of Philistia (cf. 1 Sam. 6:17). The omission of Gath apparently reflects its decline into insignificance (2 Chron. 26:6). The overthrow of Tyre fills Ashkelon, Gaza, and Ekron with dread. Not even the king will be spared at Gaza. Ashdod will be inhabited by a mixed population (cf. Neh. 13:23-24), and thus will be destroyed their pride of nationality (9:6).

Verse 7 reveals that the purpose of Yahweh's campaign is not the destruction of foreign peoples but their conversion (cf. 8:20-22; 14:16-19). The removal of "blood" and "detestable things" refers to the cessation of unlawful and idolatrous practices (Lev. 17:14; Isa. 65:4; 66:17). The converted Philistines will then be incorporated into the people of Judah. As the Jebusites of Jerusalem were absorbed by Israel (2 Sam. 24:18), Ekron and the Philistines will become part of God's people (cf. Eph. 2:13-14).

Verse 8 reveals the goal toward which Yahweh's campaign is directed. Having subjugated the nations, He returns as a victorious warrior to His Temple ("My house"). The "Divine Warrior Hymns" in ancient Near Eastern literature reflect the view that the key to protecting the newly conquered territory is maintenance of the Temple precincts.[8] Yahweh will camp around His Temple as a guard against any alien army that may tramp through Judah's territory (cf. 2:5). No oppressor

8. Hanson, "Zechariah 9 and Ancient Ritual Pattern," pp. 50-51.

will bring violence to the people for God has taken note of their distress. The anthropomorphic expression "For now I have seen with My eyes" likens God to one who has previously only heard, but now is an eyewitness of Israel's distress.

THE VICTORY SHOUT AND PROCESSION (9:9)

In verse 9 the triumphant return of the Victor to His Temple is heralded with a victory shout. The people of Jerusalem, personified as the "daughter of Zion! . . . daughter of Jerusalem!" are exhorted to rejoice and shout aloud. The reason for such shouts of joy is the arrival of their King. The messianic King theme is developed throughout the prophets (Isa. 9:6, 7; 11:1-5; Hos. 3:4-5; Amos 9:11, 12; Mic. 5:2-4). That Yahweh is the warrior and His Son serves as king presents no problem if understood in the context of ancient Near Eastern royal ideology. The "divine" king and His anointed ruler are celebrated together. So Yahweh's victory is celebrated by the procession of His Anointed.

The King is described as "just" or "righteous" (cf. Isa. 9:7; 11:4-5; 32:1). He will uphold what is right in the exercise of His royal authority. The second attribute of the King is that He is "endowed with salvation." This may mean that He has experienced deliverance, hence is victorious, or that He shows Himself a Savior of others. The third quality mentioned is His humility (cf. Phil. 2:5-8). The word *humble* suggests the condition of one who is brought low through affliction, poverty, or persecution (cf. Isa. 53:7).

The reference to the King's riding on a donkey has led many to contrast the lowliness of the ass with the pomp and splendor of a horse. But the "ass" or "donkey" was not considered a lowly creature in the ancient Near East. It was the mount of princes (Judg. 5:10; 10:4; 12:14) and kings (2 Sam. 16:1-2). Both Asherah and Baal are depicted in ancient literature as riding on donkeys. The donkey appears to have been the royal mount in the ancient Near East. Any further significance in the fact that the King rides a donkey rather than a horse is probably because of a prophetic bias against the horse and chariot as representing sinful self-reliance, that is, trust in man's weapons rather than in God's power to deliver (cf. Deut. 17:16; Ps. 33:16-17; Isa. 31:1). The King will come as a royal personage, not as a conqueror riding a war horse. The last line of verse 9 defines more exactly the words "on a donkey."

Matthew records a fulfillment of this prophecy in the life of King Jesus took place at His royal entry into Jerusalem (cf. Matt. 21:2-7; John 12:12-15). Matthew reports that the disciples brought both the donkey and the colt to Jesus (Matt. 21:7). He entered Jerusalem riding on the "young" animal (John 12:14).

THE INAUGURATION OF MESSIAH'S REIGN (9:10)

The messianic kingdom is inaugurated in verse 10 with the destruction of the weapons of war—chariot, horse, and battle bow (cf. Isa. 9:4-6). The name "Ephraim" is used to denote the ten northern tribes. The reference to both Ephraim and Jerusalem reflects the prophetic anticipation of seeing the two kingdoms reunited (cf. 8:13; Ezek. 37:15-28). After the implements of war are banished from the land, the King Messiah will "speak peace to the nations." He will establish and maintain a just and lasting peace by His sovereign rule (cf. Isa. 2:4; Mic. 4:3). The universal scope of His rule is reflected in the words "from sea to sea" (from the Mediterranean to the Persian Gulf) and "from the River to the ends of the earth" (from the Euphrates to the farthest known reaches of the southwest, cf. Ps. 72:8).

THE RELEASE OF CAPTIVES (9:11-13)

As in the "Divine Warrior Hymn" recorded in Isaiah 52:7-12, the proclamation of kingship is followed by the release of captives. The release announced here would serve as tremendous encouragement to the exiles yet in Babylon. It is on the basis of His unconditional covenant with Abraham, ratified by blood (Gen. 15:9-11), that Yahweh intervenes in behalf of His captive people. The word "prisoners" reflects the status of the Jews in exile. The "waterless pit" probably refers to a dry cistern used as a dungeon (cf. Jer. 38:6, 9).

In verse 12 the liberated captives are exhorted to return to the "stronghold," an apparent reference to Zion, which Yahweh, the Divine Warrior, secured (9:8). The Lord promises to "restore double" to His people to compensate for past sorrow. The double share was the privilege of the firstborn (Deut. 21:17). It probably refers here to a full measure of blessing and prosperity.

Verse 13 contains a bold figure in which Yahweh is depicted as fashioning Judah and Ephraim into a bow and arrow. Using similar imagery in the last line, the Lord declares that He will make the sons of Zion like a warrior's sword. The imagery suggests the sovereign control of Yahweh over His people. The reference to "Greece" (literally, "Javan") as the enemy to be overcome has been regarded as an allusion to the conflict between the Maccabees and the Greek rulers of Syria. On that basis, many would give Zechariah a late date. But the name "Javan" is applied in Genesis 20:2, 4 and Isaiah 66:19 to nations on the edge of civilization. D. R. Jones argues that "Javan" is used here as a symbol of the nations rather than as a specific reference to Greece[9] (see the Introduction, pp. 6-7).

THE THEOPHANY OF THE DIVINE WARRIOR (9:14)

Based on Israel's experience with God at Sinai (Ex. 19:16-19), the Old Testament contains many theophanies, or appearances of God. These appearances were often accompanied by thunder, lightning, smoke, and earthquakes (cf. Judg. 5:4-5; 2 Sam. 22:8-18; Pss. 29:3-9; 68:7-8; Hab. 3:3-15). Yahweh is depicted in verse 14 as sending forth arrows like lightning and blowing His ram's horn ("trumpet"). Whereas Baal is customarily depicted as riding the clouds, here Yahweh marches on the southern storm wind. The

9. D. R. Jones, "A Fresh Interpretation of Zechariah IX-XI," *Vetus Testamentum* 12 (July 1962): 248.

theophany reveals Yahweh's sovereignty and power to protect His own.

THE VICTORY BANQUET (9:15)

It is an error to regard verse 15 as recording Israel's vengeance on their enemies—eating their flesh and drinking their blood (cf. Deut. 32:35). The verse simply records the victory banquet of God's people. In celebration of Yahweh's victory over the nations and the securing of His house at Zion, the people will enjoy a feast. The word *devour* simply means "to eat." To "eat" and "drink" is a metaphor of celebration (cf. Eccles. 2:24; 5:18; 9:7). The celebrants will trample under foot the "sling stones"—useless remnants of previous conflicts. The last two lines are quite compact and suggest the extent of the eating and drinking. The lines literally read, "And they will be filled like a basin, like the corners of the altar." The people will be filled with drink like a sacrificial basin and filled with meat like the corners of a sacrificial altar.

THE RESTORATION OF PROSPERITY (9:16-17)

The first part of verse 16 summarizes what God will do for His people. As a shepherd cares for his flock, so Yahweh will save His people. The reason for this special care is the preciousness of the flock. They are to Him as jewels in a crown. The words *in His land* suggest Israel's security. As a flock is secure in the shepherd's sheepfold, so God's people are safe in His land.

Verse 17 contemplates the future blessing on God's people. The abundance of grain and wine suggests the prosperity of the coming age (Deut. 33:28; Isa. 30:23; Amos 9:13; Joel 3:18). Grain will make the young men strong, and wine will make the maidens fruitful.

THE PLAN FOR RESTORATION (10:1-12)

In the next section of Zechariah, the prophet describes how Yahweh will restore His people to their land. God will give

His people strength to overcome their oppressors (10:3), and then Yahweh Himself will restore His scattered people (vv. 6, 8-10). The unifying theme of this section is the restoration of the Jewish people by God's divine power.

THE PROSPERITY FROM THE LORD (10:1-2)

The prosperity predicted in 9:17 is dependent on the Lord, who alone blesses the land with rain. Verse 1 contains a command and a promise. The people are commanded to request rain from Yahweh—the One who "makes the storm clouds." The "spring rain" is a reference to the "latter rain" (Deut. 11:14) that comes in late spring and is so essential for causing the heads of grain to swell and providing an abundant crop. The accompanying promise assures those who pray that God will provide sufficient rain to water the crops of each man's field. God is ready and able to meet the need of those who request.

But man in his fallen state has often sought false gods in place of the true. Verse 2 reveals the folly of resorting to idols. Unlike Yahweh, man-made images cannot answer prayer. Those who worship such deities are led like aimless sheep to their own destruction. The "teraphim" were household idols (Gen. 31:19; Judg. 17:5). Like Balaam, "diviners" interpreted omens (often the vital organs of animals) as a means of foretelling the future (Josh. 13:22; 1 Sam. 6:2). The diviners represented here offered only lies, empty dreams, and unfulfilled promises. The results ("Therefore") of this lack of spiritual leadership is graphically illustrated. The people are likened to a wandering flock of sheep without a shepherd. The concept of "shepherd" is used in the ancient Near East to represent a ruler or king (cf. Ezek. 34:6-8, 23-24).

THE OVERTHROW OF THE OPPRESSORS (10:3-7)

The first two lines of verse 3 provide the key idea for this section. Continuing the "shepherd" imagery of verse 2, the

Lord declares that His "anger is kindled against the shepherds" who have abused the flock of Israel. While Israel suffered a lack of national leadership, there were plenty of
foreign tyrants who sought dominion over God's people. The
Lord declares that He will punish the "male goats"—an un-
complimentary extension of the shepherd imagery (Ezek.
34:17).

The last two lines of verse 3 summarize the means by which
God will punish foreign tyrants. He will do so by transform-
ing His shepherdless sheep into magnificent war horses!
While Yahweh will visit the tyrants with punishment, He will
"visit" the house of Judah with deliverance (cf. Ex. 3:16;
4:31). It is significant that they are likened to "His" horses.
God will strengthen the people as His instruments to overthrow the oppressors. There is a strong emphasis throughout
this chapter that the overthrow and deliverance is something
that God will accomplish (cf. 10:6, 8, 10, 12).

Verse 4 continues the use of metaphor to describe the
stability and strength God imparts to Israel. The words
"From them" (literally, "from him") have been taken to
refer to either Judah or the Lord.[10] The nearest antecedent to
the pronoun "him" is Judah. Ultimately, it is God who
brings these blessings Israel's way.

The "cornerstone" suggests steadfast strength or stability
and is used figuratively for "ruler" in Isaiah 19:13. In Psalm
118:22 it is used of the rejected Messiah. The "tent peg" suggests something (or someone) on which much depends. A peg
firmly in place implies endurance. This imagery is used in
Isaiah 22:23 to describe Eliakim the son of Hilkiah, who was
entrusted with governmental leadership. The "bow of battle"
suggests strength for military conquest (2 Kings 13:17). The
last line of verse 4 has been interpreted to mean that Judah
will be a source of future leaders, or that through God's empowerment of His people every oppressor will be driven out
of Israel.

---

10. Feinberg, *God Remembers*, p. 143.

Verse 5 predicts Judah's victory by God's empowerment. Judah will be as a nation of "mighty men," or seasoned warriors. So empowered will they be by Yahweh's might that even the dreaded cavalry will be defeated to the point of shame. Many have interpreted this verse with reference to the Maccabean victory over the Syrians, but the context of this section is more general and eschatological.

Verse 6 reveals the key to Israel's victory. The Lord declares, "And I shall strengthen the house of Judah, and I shall save the house of Joseph." The victory is the Lord's. As the "house of Judah" represents the southern territory of Israel, the "house of Joseph" represents the northern territory—Ephraim and Manasseh, Joseph's sons (Gen. 41:51-52). The words "And I shall bring them back" apply to both the northern tribes taken captive by Assyria and the people of the southern territories taken captive by Babylon. The restoration is based on God's "compassion" and is in response to their prayers for deliverance (cf. Ex. 2:23-25; Lev. 26:40-45). So complete will be their restoration that it will be as though the Exile had never taken place.

What God promised Judah in verse 5, He promises Ephraim in verse 7. Ephraim, too, will be empowered "like a mighty man [warrior]." The renewed evidence of God's concern for the northern tribes will cause those people to rejoice. This joy is abundant ("as if from wine," cf. Ps. 104:15) with its source in Yahweh ("in the LORD," cf. John 15:11).

THE REGATHERING TO THE LAND (10:8-12)

The rest of Zechariah 10 develops God's promise to regather His scattered people. Some commentators believe that these verses detail the future of the Northern Kingdom, represented by "Ephraim" (10:7). However, the text does not appear to limit the promise of regathering to Ephraim. God will bring both "Judah" and "Joseph" back to their land (10:6). These verses would, however, be especially encouraging to the Jews of the Northern Kingdom, for whereas Judah had experienced a measure of restoration under the decree of

Cyrus, the ten northern tribes were still in exile.

In verse 8 the Lord declares that He will "whistle" for His people after the manner that a shepherd signals His sheep (cf. Judg. 5:16). The reason for this regathering of God's people is explained by the phrase "For I have redeemed them." A complete redemption implies not only deliverance from sin (3:4, 9) but also deliverance from the bondage of captivity. Not only will the people be regathered, but they will be "as numerous as they were before." Before what? Apparently the reference is to before the Exile. When the Lord restores and regathers His people, their population will be as great as ever.

The Lord acknowledges in verse 9 that the Exile was His doing (cf. Deut. 28:63-64). The Lord anticipates that the people in exile "will remember Me," apparently a reference to their turning to the Lord in repentance (cf. Lev. 26:40-42; Deut. 30:1-3). Not only will the parents and children return to the land ("come back"), but, we are told, they "will live." The words "will live" imply something more than mere survival (cf. Hab. 2:4). They imply a life of blessing and may allude to the impartation of spiritual life (cf. 10:12; Ezek. 37:14).

In verse 10 the Lord names the geographical regions of captivity and identifies the lands to which the people will return. "Egypt" and "Assyria" are principal lands of Israel's captivity (Isa. 11:11; Hos. 11:11). "Assyria" may be used here in a general sense to refer to the lands of the north, including Babylon. Others suppose the word is used here because of the previous reference to "Ephraim" (10:7). The lands of "Gilead" and "Lebanon" are east and west of the Jordan respectively and are representative of the whole land of Israel. Using exaggeration (hyperbole) for emphasis, the Lord declares that so complete will the restoration be, that the territory of Israel will not be sufficient for their numbers.

Verse 11 declares that the Lord Himself will overcome the obstacles and impediments to Israel's return. Here the imagery of the Exodus is appropriated to illustrate the greatness of the obstacles and the power of God to overcome them. As

God brought His people across the Red ("Reed") Sea and the Jordan River (Ex. 14:21-32; Josh. 3:14-17), so the "sea of distress" and "depths of the Nile" will not prevent Israel's regathering. The "Nile" may be a poetic or figurative reference to the Euphrates River (cf. Isa. 11:15). The humiliation of Assyria and Egypt is emphasized in the last two lines of verse 11. The "scepter" is an emblem of governmental authority.

The thought of verse 12 is crucial to an understanding of this promise of regathering. First, it is something that will be accomplished by God's power as He gives strength to His people. The Lord's strength will enable them to overcome the obstacles and accomplish the return (cf. Phil. 4:13). Second, Israel will return to the land as a believing nation—a redeemed people (cf. 10:8). The figure of walking in the name of the Lord is used in Micah 4:5 with reference to the people in Messiah's kingdom. Thus the regathering to the Lord is an event yet future for Israel and will take place when the Jewish people have accepted their Messiah and have appropriated the blessings of the New Covenant (cf. 12:10—13:3; Rom. 11:26). Isaiah describes this return as a "second" regathering (11:11-16) that culminates in millennial worship (12:1-6).

THE REJECTION OF THE GOOD SHEPHERD (11:1-17)

Chapter 11 records prophetically the rejection of the good shepherd by God's flock, Israel, and His replacement by a worthless shepherd who brings ruin. Zechariah has been said to be one of the most difficult books of the Bible to interpret, and chapter 11 stands as no exception to that judgment.

THE CONSEQUENCES OF REJECTION (11:1-3)

Commentators are divided as to whether verses 1-3 of chapter 11 are linked more closely with the last part of chapter 10 or the first part of chapter 11. Those who view this short lyric poem as connected with chapter 11 see it as a poetic portrayal of judgment on Assyria and Egypt (10:10), represented by the cedars of Lebanon. It is suggested that Zechariah drew this imagery from Ezekiel 31:3-9 and Isaiah 10:33-34. Others link the poem with chapter 11, suggesting that it depicts the devastation of the land of Israel because of their rejection of Messiah, the good shepherd (11:4-14). Although both views have merit, it seems that the words of 10:12 serve as a fitting climax and conclusion to the previous section. Certainly the reference to the "shepherds' wail" (11:3) is more closely connected with the shepherd imagery of 11:4-17. Perhaps these verses serve as an introduction to chapter 11, setting forth in vivid poetic terms the consequences of rejecting the good shepherd.

The poem begins with a dramatic call for lofty and inaccessible Lebanon to open its doors to invaders who will set her famed cedars to the torch. In verse 2 the devastation reaches farther south, and the "oaks of Bashan" are called to lament. Bashan, noted for its fine pastures, was the northern territory of Israel east of the Jordan. The devastating judgment reaches even farther south in verse 3 and touches the "pride of the Jordan." This phrase may be translated "jungle of the Jordan," a reference to the thick growth of trees and shrubs that fringe the banks of the Jordan and provide shelter for wild beasts.

The great thrust of this passage is the wailing that reflects the horror of the devastation. The cypress (or "juniper") and oaks wail for the cedars of Lebanon. The shepherds wail for the ruin of Bashan. And the young lions roar for the destruction of Jordan's jungle. In this poetic passage, Lebanon, Bashan, and the Jordan River appear to represent the entire land of Israel. As with most invasions of Israel, the devastation begins in the north and proceeds south.

What historical event in Israel's past or prophetic history could this passage refer to? The poem is linked closely with the rejection of the good shepherd (11:4-14) and serves to introduce that rejection. Although the passage itself is too general a description of judgment to be conclusive, it may be linked with the judgment Jesus pronounced on Israel because of the Jewish leaders' rejection of Him (Matt. 23:37-39). It is possible that the judgment anticipated here was fulfilled with the Roman subjugation of Israel and destruction of Jerusalem and the Temple (A.D. 70). The obvious difficulty with this view is the lack of reference in these verses to the destruction of Jerusalem. But this omission may not be significant in a highly poetic passage of this nature.

THE DESTINY OF THE SHEPHERD AND FLOCK (11:4-14)

Zechariah 11:4-14 has been labeled "the most enigmatic" prophecy in the Old Testament.[11] The passage speaks of a shepherd who looks after a flock doomed to be slaughtered. The flock represents Israel, and the shepherd represents a divinely appointed leader who was rejected by his people. Severe judgment results from Israel's rejection of this good shepherd.[12]

In verse 4 the Lord commissions Zechariah to pasture the flock of His people Israel. It may be that Zechariah was to act out a symbolic action like other prophets (cf. Mic. 1:8), but the involvement of the "three shepherds" (11:8) and the people (11:2) suggest that the narrative records something more like a parable or an allegory. The extended and detailed nature of the comparison would point to the latter. The flock is depicted as sheep destined for slaughter. The ruthless leaders of Israel were not caring for the people as if they desired them to live.

Verse 5 extends the imagery of the worthless shepherds who had merely used the flock of Israel to their own economic advantage. As sheep raised only to provide meat, so God's people were suffering under the oppression of sheep merchants interested only in self-enrichment. Like the hireling, they had no genuine concern for the sheep (John 10:13). "Those who buy them" may refer to the foreign rulers who trafficked in

---

11. S. R. Driver, "Minor Prophets II," *Century Bible* (1906), p. 253.
12. See Jones, "A Fresh Interpretation of Zechariah IX-XI," 250-55, for a helpful analysis.

Jewish captives (Amos 1:6). "Their own shepherds" refers to the Jewish leaders who failed to express compassionate concern for their own people. They have abandoned true pastoral care (cf. 1 Pet. 5:2).

The Lord speaks in verse 6 and reveals the destiny of His flock Israel. "For I shall no longer have pity on the inhabitants of the land," declares Yahweh. The results of Zechariah's assignment is negative from the outset (cf. Isa. 6:9-13). The judgment on the worthless leaders of Israel ("shepherds," v. 5) is somewhat ironic. They will "fall . . . into one another's power and into the power of his king." The wicked leaders of Israel will find themselves the powerless victims of others. "They will strike the land" speaks of the foreign kings whom God will allow to overtake and ruin the petty tyrants' land. Their end is decreed. God will not rescue the petty tyrants from the power of the attacking kings.

In obedience to Yahweh's command, Zechariah pastured the flock destined for the slaughterhouse (11:7). The words "hence the afflicted of the flock" are debated. Following the Hebrew text, the words are taken to refer to the poor or wretched ones of the flock. Following the Septuagint version's "for the Canaanites," the reference appears to be to "sheep merchants" (as "Canaanite" bears the meaning "merchant" in Ezekiel 16:29 and 17:4). It is argued that the Septuagint gives the more difficult reading (and therefore preferred reading) and that the context shows that the Septuagint's reading fits better than that of the Masoretic text.[13] The idea of the phrase would be that Zechariah shepherds the flock for the "sheep merchants," who do the slaughtering. Whether or not the Septuagint records the best reading of verse 11, the idea of "sheep merchants" is certainly not foreign to the passage (cf. 11:5, 12).

As shepherds carried implements to guide and protect the

13. Thomas J. Finley, "The Sheep Merchants of Zechariah 11," *Grace Theological Journal* 3 (Spring 1982): 51-65.

sheep (cf. Ps. 23:4), so Zechariah has two staffs—one named "Favor" or "Grace" and the other called "Union." The naming of the staffs gives insight into the aim of Zechariah's ministry as a shepherd. He wanted the flock to enjoy God's favor and to experience national unity. Zechariah was obedient to his pastoral commission, but his hope for Israel was not to be realized.

Verse 8 is extremely problematic. Essentially it reflects the diligence with which Zechariah carried out his pastoral duties and the rejection of the shepherd by his flock. At least forty different conjectures have been offered as to the identity of the three shepherds that Zechariah deposed. The translation "annihilated" is a bit strong. The shepherds were "cut off" in the sense of being dismissed, not necessarily put to death. The three shepherds have been thought to represent three classes of rulers in Israel—kings, priest, and prophets—all of which proved unfaithful. Others have identified them as three leaders who lost their positions in rapid succession—the last three kings of Israel, the last three kings of Judah, or certain high priests of the Maccabean period. The diversity of opinions suggests that it is not possible to identify the shepherds with certainty. In spite of the definite article ("the" three shepherds), which encourages speculation as to their identity, such guesswork is both unwise and unnecessary. The shepherds were leaders in Israel who did not share the good shepherd's vision. Thus they were removed from their positions of leadership. The "one month" may refer to a literal thirty-day period or indicate that the removals took place in a relatively short time (cf. Hos. 5:7).

As Zechariah the shepherd came to the end of his patience in dealing with the flock, so also the people became "weary" of him. The word translated *weary* is a strong term for rejection and suggests that Zechariah was "loathed" or "detested." In response to their rejection of the good shepherd, Zechariah abandoned the flock to its fate ("I will not pasture you"). The words of verse 9 "What is to die, let it die," announce the well-deserved judgment on the flock.

Cannibalism ("eat one another's flesh") was one of the horrors of famine resulting from siege warfare (Deut. 28:54-57; Lam. 4:10; Josephus, *War* VI. 201-13).

Verse 10 records the breaking of the staff "Favor," symbolic of the termination of God's gracious dealings with His people. Their rejection of the shepherd meant judgment instead of blessing. The breaking of "my covenant" has been variously interpreted. Some would suggest that the covenant, represented by the staff, was with the people of Israel. Thus, God broke His covenant with His people. But what covenant would God break? Certainly God would not break His unconditional promise to Abraham (Gen. 12:1-3) or to David (2 Sam. 7:12-16). The conditional Mosaic covenant (Ex. 19-24) had already been broken by Israel's disobedience. The promises given in 8:11-13, 14-15, 19-23 appear inconsistent with the view that God will yet break a covenant with Israel. It is more likely that the covenant mentioned here is one with the Gentile nations ("all the peoples") in Israel's behalf. This covenant may involve a divine restraint being placed on the nations to prevent them from harming Israel. This would be similar to the covenant of peace mentioned in Ezekiel 34:25 (cf. Hos. 2:18). The breaking of the covenant meant that Israel was no longer protected. That latter view is favored by the context and a proper understanding of God's covenant dealings with Israel.

Verse 11 records the reaction of those who witnessed the symbolic breaking of Zechariah's staff. The words "afflicted of the flock" are identical with the words in verse 7, which some have understood to refer to "sheep merchants".[14] The observers of Zechariah's symbolic action immediately realized that it had prophetic import. The breaking of the covenant of protection was by divine design. It was the manifestation of God's judgment on the people who rejected His appointed shepherd.

In verse 12 Zechariah the shepherd requests wages for the

14. Ibid.

service he had rendered. Because Zechariah had terminated the contract (11:9), his request is rather hesitant: "If it is good in your sight." It is debated as to whether he addresses the whole flock or just the sheep merchants. If "the afflicted of the flock" (11:7, 11) is better read "sheep merchants," then there is no doubt. The prophet is to be paid off by the sheep traders. But even if the Septuagint reading is rejected, the thought of "sheep merchants" is intrinsic to the context (11:5, 12).

The authorities calculated Zechariah's wages to be thirty pieces (i.e., shekels) of silver—the price of a gored slave (Ex. 21:32). This valuation occurs in the Sumarian "The Curse of Agade" as a sign of contempt.[15] This was the price Judas received from the Jewish authorities for the betrayal of Jesus (Matt. 26:15; 27:9). The fact that Matthew attributes this prophecy to Jeremiah rather than Zechariah may be attributed to his combining Zechariah 11:12-13 with Jeremiah 18:1-4 and 32:6-9. Following contemporary literary custom, he cites the name of the more prominent prophet.

Verse 13 reflects Yahweh's response to the valuation of His shepherd. With a note of sarcasm, Zechariah is instructed to ask the "magnificent price" of his service to the potter in the Temple. It is noted that the wages of Zechariah are considered by the Lord to reflect the people's valuation of Him. Indeed, Zechariah was God's appointed shepherd. In one's Christology, the value one places on Christ reflects how highly one appreciates the Father (cf. John 15:21, 23-24).

On the basis of the similarity between the Hebrew words for "potter" and "treasury," some have followed the Syriac translation emending verse 13 to read "throw it into the treasury." However, such emendation is unnecessary. It is possible that the expression "throw it to the potter" is simply a proverbial expression of contempt like "throw it away." The verse clearly indicates that the money was cast into the

---

15. James B. Prichard, ed., *Ancient Near Eastern Texts,* 3d ed. (Princeton: Princeton U., 1969), p. 648, line 104.

Temple. On the other hand, potters were connected with the Temple because of the continual need for sacrificial vessels (Lev. 6:28). It has been suggested that there may have been a guild of potters who served the Temple (cf. Jer. 18:6; 19:1).[16] Whatever the case, the thirty pieces of silver were flung into the Temple. Because Judas's wages represented "blood money," they could not be used for Temple service and were used for the purchase of a potter's field as a burial place for strangers (cf. Matt. 27:6-10).

The prophet's next symbolic action was the destruction of his staff, "Union" (11:14). Because of their rejection of the good shepherd, the national unity Zechariah hoped for would not be achieved at this time. Yet Ezekiel prophesied a day when Israel and Judah would be reunited under the leadership of one Shepherd (Ezek. 37:16-28).

THE APPOINTMENT OF A WORTHLESS SHEPHERD (11:15-17)

The rejection of the leadership of Yahweh's personal representative leads to the appointment of a worthless shepherd—a shepherd of doom. A vacuum of spiritual leadership is often quickly filled by those whose interests in God's flock is motivated by selfish considerations. In verse 15 Zechariah is commanded to take up the equipment of a "foolish" or "worthless" shepherd. The equipment mentioned here would probably be no different from that of the good shepherd. The difference lies in the respective attitudes of the two shepherds toward the flock.

The symbolic action of Zechariah is explained by the Lord in verse 16. Yahweh declares that He will raise up a shepherd who will not only neglect his shepherding duties but will actually destroy the flock! The failure of this shepherd in terms of pastoral care for the sheep recalls the words of Ezekiel 34:3-4. The words "devour the flesh" and "tear off their hoofs" are graphic expressions of the savagery of the worthless shepherd.

16. Baldwin, *Haggai, Zechariah, Malachi,* p. 186.

Verse 17 describes the fate of the foolish shepherd. The worthless shepherd who abandons his flock is to be judged. The Lord declares that "a sword will be on his arm and on his right eye!" As a result, the arm that should have protected the sheep will be withered, and the eye that should have watched over the flock will be blinded. The worthless shepherd is not identified in the text. Most Jewish commentators see a fulfillment in King Herod (63-4 B.C.), noted for his harsh dealings with the Jews. Others suggest Alcimus (163-159 B.C.), the high priest who treacherously betrayed the Maccabees (1 Macc. 7:1-25). A comparison of his person and work with the sinister figure of Daniel 7:25-27 and 11:36-39 points to the view that he represents the Antichrist (cf. 2 Thess. 2:1-12; Rev. 13:1-10).

5

THE ORACLE CONCERNING ISRAEL'S FUTURE

(ZECHARIAH 12-14)

Chapters 12-14 repeat the themes of judgment, deliverance, and blessing observed in Zechariah 9-11 and bring them to a climax. This section is consistently eschatological in content and reveals a great deal concerning Messiah's second coming and the establishment of His kingdom. Repetition of the phrase "in that day" occurring seventeen times in these chapters stirs anticipation for the Day of the Lord with its culmination in Israel's repentance and the inauguration of God's universal kingdom.

THE PHYSICAL DELIVERANCE OF THE NATION (12:1-9)

Chapters 12-14 begin as did chapters 9-11, "The burden of the word of Yahweh." However, whereas the previous section concerned the Gentile nations, these chapters relate God's future dealings with His covenant people Israel. Again, the word "burden" is used in an ominous sense; a weighty judgment that the prophet must discharge. Although "Israel" often refers to the northern tribes, here it is used in a general sense for Judah and Jerusalem.

In verse 1 the prophet uses three phrases to describe the greatness of Yahweh. The first two highlight God's Word in creating the universe and planet Earth. The third phrase focuses on the climax of God's creative work, the creation of man and woman (Gen. 1:26-28). The "spirit [or "breath"] of man" refers to an immaterial aspect of man's being that gives him life and vitality (cf. Gen 2:7). The threefold description of God may reflect Isaiah 42:5. By rehearsing Yahweh's works of the past, Zechariah assures his readers of God's ability to fulfill the promises about to be revealed.

Verse 2 begins with the word "Behold," which draws attention to an unusual situation. Jerusalem is depicted as a cup of wine or strong drink that causes those who drink from it to stagger about. The "cup" as a metaphor of the wrath of God is found in both the Old and New Testaments (Isa. 51:17; Jer. 25:15; Ezek. 23:33; Rev. 14:10; 16:19). The judgment to befall Jerusalem's attackers will occur in the context of a siege. In a military assault, a siege is designed to isolate and deprive the enemy of supplies, thereby bringing about surrender with as little cost as possible for the attacker. The extent of Jerusalem's future siege is revealed in verse 3: "And all the nations of the earth will be gathered against it." The cup of God's wrath will cause Israel's attackers to stagger and fall when they mount a siege against Jerusalem.

The last phrase of verse 2, "It will also be against Judah," has been interpreted by many to indicate that Judah will participate in the siege, either by choice or by the compulsion of the attackers. According to this view Judah will then turn its arms against the nations upon realizing that God is fighting for Jerusalem. But this interpretation involves more hypothesis than exegesis. A Judean attack on Jerusalem would be unthinkable (cf. 12:5). The words simply reveal that the siege that affects Jerusalem will also affect Judah. The two will share a common fate. An attack on Jerusalem would involve the invasion of Judah.

Verse 3 uses a different metaphor to describe God's judgment on those who would attack Jerusalem. The city is likened to a "heavey stone" that brings severe injury to those who would attempt to remove it from its place. As overexertion results in bodily injury, so also attempts to harm Jerusalem will result in severe judgment on the attackers. The metaphors of the cup and the stone graphically illustrate the truth that those who would harm God's covenant people bring upon themselves the curse of God (Gen. 12:3; Zech. 2:8).

In verse 4 Yahweh reveals how He will intervene for Jerusalem in that eschatological "day" of judgment. He will confound both the horse and horsemen of the besieging army while He watches over the people of Judah with care. It is quite clear that deliverance comes by God's power ("I will . . . I will"), not through the military prowess of Judah. The Lord's watchcare over Judah is graphically depicted by God's words "I will watch over [open My eyes upon] the house of Judah." The threefold judgment of madness, blindness, and bewilderment also appears in the curses of the covenant (Deut. 28:28).

Seeing the intervention of God for His people will cause the leaders of Judah to affirm God's power to deliver through His people. The NASB's "clans" (v. 5) literally means "ruler of a thousand" and is better translated "chiefs" or "leaders."[1] They express the confidence of Judah in the words, "A strong support for us are the inhabitants of Jerusalem." The qualifying statement, "through the LORD of hosts, their God," gives recognition to the Lord as the ultimate source of power for victory (Dan. 11:32; Phil. 4:13).

Verse 6 reveals how God will empower the "clans" or "leaders" of Judah to turn on the Gentile foes in their midst. Two metaphors of destruction are used. Judah is first likened to a "firepot" among pieces of wood. A firepot was a pottery vessel used to carry hot coals for the purpose of building a fire. The coals would quickly ignite a pile of dry twigs into a blazing fire. The second metaphor is that of a flaming torch among the sheaves of grain. Standing grain would quickly be consumed by a blaze (cf. Judg. 15:4-5). In a similar manner the leaders of Judah will consume the attackers on both

---

1. *Theological Wordbook of the Old Testament,* ed. R. L. Harris, Gleason L. Archer, and Bruce K. Waltke, s.v. *'allup,* by J. B. Scott (Chicago: Moody, 1981), 1:48.

flanks. As a consequence, the siege against Jerusalem will be lifted, and the city will remain settled on her site as before the attack.

Verse 7 reveals that God's deliverance will first come to the "tents of Judah"—the Jews dwelling in rural districts. God's purpose in delivering Judah first is to prevent "the glory of the house of David and the glory of the inhabitants of Jerusalem" from being exalted above Judah. The "house of David" refers to David's descendants who share the honor of his name. The "inhabitants of Jerusalem" share in the glorious reputation of that city. Because the Jews living in the country apparently thought of themselves as less privileged than those living in Jerusalem, God honors Judah by delivering her first and thus discourages rivalry or division among the Jewish people. Paul applied the same principle to dealings within the Body of Christ (1 Cor. 12:22-25). The deliverance of defenseless Judah before the fortified and well-defended capital will demonstrate to all that the victory is from the Lord.[2]

Verse 8 further describes the divine deliverance of Jerusalem mentioned in verse 5. God will defend the city by enabling even her feeble soldiers to stand firm like David, the great warrior and national hero (cf. Ps. 18:36). The "house of David," a reference to David's royal family and descendants, will be "like God," who is renowned as a mighty warrior (Ex. 15:2). That bold analogy, likening David's descendants to God, is climaxed in the next phrase, "like the angel of the LORD." The same comparison was often made with David himself (1 Sam. 29:9; 2 Sam. 14:17, 20; 19:27). The "angel of the LORD" in the Old Testament, quite clearly a divine being (cf. Ex. 23:20; Josh. 5:1; Judg. 13:15-22), is identified as the preincarnate Christ. Great power is available to those who fully commit themselves to God's work (Acts 1:8).

Verse 9 reveals that God is planning a "search and destroy" mission. When the hostile Gentile nations come up

2. Feinberg, *God Remembers,* p. 175.

against Jerusalem, He will "set about to destroy the nations." Does "set about" or "seek" imply that the mission may be unsuccessful? More in keeping with the thought of the narrative is the idea of priority or focus. God will concentrate His full attention on the destruction of Israel's enemies even as a marksman must give his undivided attention to hitting the target. The words "all nations" must be understood in the context to refer to representative armies of the attacking nations (cf. 14:16).

THE SPIRITUAL RENEWAL OF THE NATION (12:10—13:6)

Zechariah now moved from the subject of Israel's physical deliverance by God's intervention to the nation's repentance and spiritual renewal. Victory over the attacking nations leads not to rejoicing but rather to mourning and a sense of remorse over Israel's rejection of their Messiah.

THE CLEANSING OF JERUSALEM (12:10—13:1)

The Lord declares in verse 10 that He will pour out on the Jewish people "the Spirit of grace and of supplication." The recipients of this outpouring include representatives of the whole nation, referred to as "the house [i.e., descendants] of David and inhabitants of Jerusalem." The expression "pour out" is a metaphor derived from the deluge of winter rains in Israel (cf. Job 36:28; Isa. 44:3; Lam. 2:19). It speaks of abundant provision. The NASB has capitalized "Spirit" and inserted an article ("the"), suggesting a reference to the Holy Spirit (cf. Heb. 10:29). Other prophetic texts support that interpretation (Isa. 32:15; Ezek. 39:29; Joel 2:28-29).

The "Spirit of grace" would be the gracious working of the Holy Spirit that leads to conviction and repentance (cf. John 16:8-11). The term *supplication* is derived from the same Hebrew word translated "grace" and suggests a prayer for grace, hence "supplication." The Spirit will stimulate an attitude of repentance and a heart cry for God's mercy. The result of the Spirit's work is revealed in the last line of the verse. With bitter grief and mourning, the Jewish people "will look upon Me whom they have pierced." Who is this one who was pierced?

It has been suggested that the reference is to some historical individual like Simon the Maccabee, who was assassinated in 134 B.C. (1 Macc. 16:11-24). John Calvin took a "metaphorical" approach, suggesting that God was "wounded" by the sins of His people, especially by their contempt for His Word.[3] Jewish commentators regard this as a corporate reference to the Jews who were slain as martyrs in the defense of Jerusalem (12:1-9). The Jewish Talmud, however, views the text with reference to the Messiah, who would be "pierced" in battle (*Sukkah* 52a). Several factors favor a messianic interpretation, the fulfillment occuring at the crucifixion of Christ. First, the mourning described is compared to that for an "only son" or a "first-born." The person of Jesus Christ certainly meets the qualification of being God's First-born; His unique, one-of-a-kind Son (John 1:18; 3:16; Rom. 8:29; Col. 1:15, 18). Second, Jesus was "pierced" with a spear by a Roman soldier after His death on the cross (John 19:34). Third, John, by divine inspiration, interpreted the piercing of Jesus to be a fulfillment of Zechariah 12:10 (cf. John 19:34-37). Fourth, in Zechariah 12:10, *God* is speaking (cf. 12:1, 4) and says, "They will look upon Me whom they have pierced." God was, in fact, "pierced" in the Person of His divine Son. Fifth, this text compares favorably with Isaiah 53:5, which mentions the piercing of Yahweh's Servant, who is none other than Jesus, the Messiah.

Although a Roman soldier actually pierced Christ's body with the lance, it was the Jews who demanded the crucifixion and accepted responsibility for the deed (cf. Matt. 27:22-25; John 19:6, 15). It should be mentioned, however, that Jesus died for the sins of both Jews and Gentiles, and that both bear responsibility for His death (Acts 2:23).

Verse 11 continues to emphasize the greatness of the

---

3. John Calvin, *Commentaries on the Twelve Minor Prophets,* (Grand Rapids: Eerdmans, 1950), 5:364; *Commentary on the Gospel According to John* (Grand Rapids: Eerdmans, 1949), 2:242.

mourning by making a further comparison. The mourning in Jerusalem will be "like the mourning of Hadadrimmon in the plain of Megiddo." It is not clear from the text whether "Hadadrimmon" is the name of a person, a god (2 Kings 5:18), or a place (Josh. 15:32; Zech. 14:10).

The mention of "Meggido" in connection with mourning is reminiscent of the death of Josiah who was mourned annually (2 Kings 23:29; 2 Chron. 35:25). "Haddad" was the name of a Canaanite storm god, and "Rimmon" was a local representation of that deity in Syria (2 Kings 5:18). "Hadadrimmon" may reflect a combination of that name. According to a Canaanite myth, Hadad, father of Aleyin, mourned his son's death at the hand of Mot. Like the weeping for Tammuz in Ezekiel 8:14, perhaps there was a ritual mourning observed by idolatrous Israelites on an annual basis. Baldwin suggests that such a festival may have been combined with mourning the death of Josiah, hence the appearance of the place name "Megiddo."[4] But would God compare the mourning for His beloved Son with that observed at a syncretistic cultic festival?

M. Delcor emends the text to read, "The mourning of that day will be like the mourning for the son of Amon [i.e., Josiah] in the plan of Megiddo."[5] This is an interesting suggestion, but highly speculative. Although there appears to be no certain solution to this enigmatic reference, the point of the passage is clear. The mourning by repentant Israel over the piercing of Messiah will be the expression of deep sorrow and intense grief.

Verses 12-14 emphasize the universal aspect of the mourning. Not only will the Jews in Jerusalem express their grief, but "the land will mourn" (12:12), including the royal family, the priestly family, and all the citizens. It has been suggested that "Nathan" refers to David's prophet (2 Sam. 7:2) and that "Shimei" is the one who cursed David (2 Sam. 16:5).

4. Baldwin, *Haggai, Zechariah, Malachi*, p. 193.
5. M. Delcor, "Duex passages difficiles: Zacharie 12:11 et 11:13," *Vetus Testamentum* 3 (1953): pp. 67-73.

A more likely view is that four family names are mentioned—two from the royal line under the names David and
his son Nathan (2 Sam. 5:14) and two from the priestly line,
Levi and his grandson Shimei. (Num. 3:18, 21). There appears to be no particular reason that the royal and priestly
families are picked out, except that they represent the nation.
The emphasis is on the fact that *all* will mourn, regardless of
office, status, or position. The repeated phrase "every family
by itself; . . . and their wives by themselves" (vv. 13-14) is
quoted in the Talmud by rabbis arguing for the separation of
men and women in worship (*Sukkah* 51*b,* 52*a*). The point of
the phrase seems to be that each will face his or her sorrow
alone, without the comfort of companionship.

The Spirit's work bringing about Israel's repentance will
result in spiritual cleansing. In 13:1 the Lord declares, "In
that day a fountain will be opened for the house of David and
for the inhabitants of Jerusalem, for sin and for impurity."
The cleansing prophesied here was illustrated in 3:3-5 in the
removal of Joshua's filthy garments. The promise of a cleansing "fountain" speaks of an abundant, copious, overflowing
provision. That the fountain will be "opened" rather than
"dug" suggests that the cleansing has been available for some
time. Like Abraham's wells, which were stopped up by the
Philistines (cf. Gen. 26:15-18), the fountain had only to be
opened for the cleansing to be appropriated. Such cleansing
was promised by Ezekiel (Ezek. 36:25-28) and constitutes a
major provision of the New Covenant (Jer. 31:31-34).

Those who will benefit from the cleansing of the fountain
are identified as "the house of David and . . . the inhabitants
of Jerusalem." As seen in 12:10-11, they represent the whole
nation of Israel—the Jewish people. The cleansing is seen to
be for the removal of "sin" and "impurity." The former is a
general term for failure in meeting God's standard; missing
the mark. The latter term is used for ritual or sexual impurity
(cf. Lev. 15:19-20, 26; Ezek. 36:17). Taken together they
speak of every deviation from God's standard—both moral
and ceremonial. The emphasis of the verse is that the cleans-

ing to be appropriated by repentant Israel will be abundantly sufficient for their forgiveness from sin and complete spiritual renewal. The "washing of regeneration and renewing by the Holy Spirit" is a yet future hope for the people of Israel (Rom. 11:26-27; Titus 3:5).

THE PURGING OF FALSE PROPHETS (13:2-6)

Despite the laws found in Deuteronomy 13:1-5 and 18:20-22, false prophets existed among the people before and during the Exile. Both Jeremiah and Ezekiel found it necessary to denounce the false prophets who were leading the people astray (Jer. 23:9-40; Ezek. 13). Zechariah announces in verses 2-6 that a day is coming when false prophets will be purged from the land along with idolatry and demonic influence.

In that future day of Israel's cleansing, Yahweh promises to "cut off the names of the idols from the land." In ancient times a person's name was the reflection of his reputation. The name represented the character or attributes of the person (cf. Matt. 1:21). Cutting off the names of the idols speaks of the utter and complete removal of both the reputation and acknowledgments of false gods. The word *idols* speaks of carved images, but Ezekiel points out the existence of idols in men's hearts (Ezek. 14:3, 7). So thorough will be the purging that the names of the idols will no longer be remembered. The names of Baal, Asherah, El, Marduk, and Dagon will be obliterated from both the minds and memories of God's people.

The Lord declares that he will also "remove the prophets and the unclean spirit from the land." The former reference is to the false prophets—those who speak lies in the name of Yahweh (cf. 13:3). The term "unclean spirit" is found only here in the Old Testament but appears frequently in the gospels (cf. Matt. 12:43; Mark 1:23) with reference to one who is demon-possessed (Luke 4:33, 36). Both false prophets and demonic influence will be banished from the land.

Because of its satanic undergirding, false prophecy dies hard. The Lord, therefore, reveals in verse 3 the severe dealings in the case of recurrence of such evil. In accordance with Deuteronomy 13:5 and 18:20, the false prophet will be put to death. The unusual thing about this judgment is that the parents will confront the false prophet and carry out the execution. The words "who gave birth to him" are repeated twice to emphasize the severity of the judgment—parents putting to death their own child! The word "pierce" (cf. 12:10) suggests the idea of being run through with a weapon (Num. 25:7-8).

Verses 4-6 depict the embarrassment and shame of those in Israel who have been involved with false prophecy. Each will be "ashamed of his vision" (v. 4). Popular opinion against the false prophets will cause them to shun every association with their occupation. The "hairy robe" that they will want to avoid was worn by Elijah (2 Kings 1:8), and appears to have been the distinctive attire of the prophets. Instead of laying claim to the office of prophet they say, "I am not a prophet; I am a tiller of the ground" (13:5). Any association with the prophetic office will be denied (cf. Amos 7:14). The claim to have been sold "as a slave in my youth" identifies one as coming from the lowest working class.

Verse 6 has been understood by some commentators to refer to Christ. It is suggested that the "wounds" received at the hands of friends correspond to the piercing of the Messiah in 12:10. That view requires a transition into a new subject between verses 5 and 6. There is no exegetical support for such a viewpoint. Never was Jesus wounded by His friends. The context of verses 4-6 relates to the matter of false prophets.

The false prophet who denies his former occupation is questioned, "What are these wounds between your arms?" The expression, "between your arms" (literally, "between your hands") refers to the body, whether the chest or back (cf. 2 Kings 9:24).[6] These wounds appear to betray the profes-

6. Baldwin, *Haggai, Zechariah, Malachi*, p. 196.

sion of an ecstatic prophet who has slashed himself on the back and breast to gain the attention and blessing of his god (cf. 2 Kings 18:28).

Under interrogation, he offers the explanation "Those with which I was wounded in the house of my friends." "Friends" has been taken as a reference to parents and friends who disciplined the man for propagating false prophecy (cf. 13:3). But the piercing mentioned in verse 3 results in death. It has also been suggested that the reference is to a brawl with one's friends that results in injury. Because the word *friends* often carries a derogatory connotation implying an idolatrous lover under the figure of spiritual adultery (cf. Jer. 22:20; Ezek. 16:33; 23:5, 9), the term may refer here to associates in idolatrous worship. Accordingly, the "house" would refer to a pagan temple.

The explanation may be understood as a denial of involvement in false prophecy or as a penitent admission by one who has received cleansing. If the former is true, the word "friend" is probably used ironically, suggesting to the reader implicit involvement in idolatrous worship.

THE FATE OF THE SHEPHERD AND HIS FLOCK (13:7-9)

Verses 7-9 focus on the purging of God's people occasioned by the death of His shepherd. This poetic section resumes the shepherd motif introduced in 11:4 and brings it to a climax. Here the shepherd is slain, and the sheep are scattered.

In verse 7 a sword, the instrument of death, is personified as a warrior and is commanded to stir to action. Yahweh speaks saying, "Awake, O sword, against My Shepherd, and against the man, My Associate." The metaphor of a shepherd was used in antiquity to refer to national leaders (cf. Ezek. 34). The "Shepherd" referred to here is a most significant leader in that Yahweh calls him "My Shepherd." Although some would identify him with the worthless shepherd of 11:15-17, his association with the Lord would indicate that he is the shepherd represented by Zechariah in 11:4-14. He is none other than the One who was "pierced" (12:10)—Jesus the Messiah. He is called God's "Associate." The term is used elsewhere of one who is a near neighbor or close companion (Lev. 6:2 [5:21 in the Hebrew Old Testament], 18:20; 19:15). It suggests a relationship of equality and calls to mind the words of Jesus in John 10:30 and 14:9 (cf. John 5:18).

After the sword is roused, it is commanded, "Strike the Shepherd." The smiting by sword recalls the piercing mentioned in 12:20. Although Jesus, the Good Shepherd, was betrayed and crucified by wicked men, it is clear from this and other texts that His death was according to the predetermined plan of God (cf. Acts 2:23). Isaiah 53:10 declares, "But the LORD was pleased to crush Him." The death of the Shepherd was according to divine plan, not the chance result of unfortunate circumstances.

The Shepherd's death results in the scattering of the sheep. Without guidance and direction from the Shepherd, the flock wanders off over the rocky and often treacherous countryside. Jesus drew His thoughts from this verse as He announced His death and the scattering of His disciples (Matt. 26:31; Mark 14:27). He identified Himself as the "good shepherd" who lays down His life for the sheep (John 10:11-18).

The last phrase of verse 7 has been interpreted by some commentators in a favorable sense suggesting that Yahweh will turn His hand to protect the helpless sheep. Yet the context suggests that the passage deals with judgment. This expression is uniformly employed in a negative or unfavorable sense (cf. Ps. 81:14; Ezek. 38:12; Amos 1:8).[7] God has sovereignly decreed that the shepherdless sheep will suffer.

Are these "little ones" Messiah's first-century disciples, unbelieving Jews, or a faithful remnant of the future? It is difficult to be certain. The disciples were definitely persecuted (John 16:1-4). Unbelieving Jews have suffered through the Jewish War, the Crusades, the Spanish Inquisition, and the

7. Merrill F. Unger, *Zechariah: The Prophet of Messiah's Glory* (Grand Rapids: Zondervan, 1963), p. 233.

Nazi Holocaust. And the faithful remnant of Israel will suffer through the Tribulation before Messiah's second coming (Matt. 24:4-31; Dan. 9:27; 12:1). Perhaps it is best to take the passages as a general prophecy of persecution and suffering for the shepherdless people of Israel rather than a promise regarding some specific group.

The thought of purging through great trial is expanded in verses 8 and 9. Verse 8 reveals the devastating result of God's dealing with the errant flock. In Israel's rugged and often barren terrain, a shepherdless flock is doomed. The Lord's hand against the land of Israel will result in the destruction of "two parts." It is obvious from the context and from verse 8 that the "parts" of the land refer to the people of the land ("them," v. 8). "Land" cannot really be "cut off and perish," but people living in the land can. The scattered flock will face a great judgment, which only one-third will survive.

As Ezekiel anticipated the survival of a remnant from the Babylonian Exile (cf. Ezek. 5:2-3), so Zechariah anticipates the Lord's deliverance of a remnant through the refiner's fire. Although two-thirds of the flock will be "cut off and perish," the one-third will be purged and purified even as the refiner's fire separates the dross from pure metal. Silver and gold are usually found in impuce states and must be heated to remove the impurities. The imagery of a smelting pot is used by other prophets to speak of the purging of sin and wickedness from God's people (Isa. 1:22, 25; Jer. 6:29-30; Ezek. 22:18-22). The term "test" appears to build on the term "refine." Once refined, precious metal must be tested or assayed to determine its value.

The result of the extreme measures taken by God with regard to His flock is reflected in the final words of the poem. The repentant people will call upon Yahweh, and He will answer them. Yahweh will acknowledge the purged and purified remnant with the words "They are My people." The redeemed of Israel will respond, "The LORD is my God." Those words speak of a covenant relationship and call to mind the words in Ezekiel 36:28 where God addresses spiritually renewed Israel: "So you will be My people, and I will be your God" (cf. 37:23, 27). Hosea anticipates a similar confession of Yahweh and His people as their covenant relationship is reestablished and renewed (Hosea. 2:23). So, too, the apostle Paul looked to that great day when "all Israel will be saved" (Rom. 11:26-27).

THE SECOND COMING OF MESSIAH (14:1-7)

Zechariah 14 describes the events that will bring to culmination this present age and inaugurate the age to come—the messianic kingdom. Verses 1-7 elaborate on the siege, defense, and deliverance of Jerusalem introduced in Zechariah 12:1-9.

Zechariah announces in verse 1, "Behold, a day is coming for the LORD when the spoil taken from you will be divided among you." That coming day is distinctively "for the LORD"—denoting His possession and authority over this future period of judgment. That day is yet future, but its coming is absolutely certain. At that time spoil will be taken from "you." Both the feminine pronouns ("you") and the context (cf. 14:2) point to the fact that "you" is Jerusalem. The spoils, or booty of war, will be divided in Jerusalem's midst. The Jewish Targum suggests that this refers to Israel's dividing the spoil of her enemies, apparently anticipating the victory mentioned in verse 14. The immediate context, however, indicates that this refers to the spoil taken from Jerusalem by her enemies (cf. 14:2).

Verse 2 explains how it is that Jerusalem will be defeated and spoiled. Yahweh declares, "For I will gather all the nations against Jerusalem to battle." The gathering of the nations against Jerusalem was announced in 12:3, but here it is revealed that Yahweh will bring it to pass. God can use even the evil actions of evil, sinful people to accomplish His sovereign purposes (cf. Gen. 50:20; Acts 2:23). The expression "all . . . nations" refers to the representative armies of the major world powers. As a result of this multinational attack, Jerusalem will be captured and plundered. As was the custom of ancient conquerors, women will be raped (Isa. 13:6) and inhabitants will be exiled (2 Kings 17:6; 24:14; 25:11). Half the population surviving the attack will be allowed to remain in Jerusalem. This group must constitute part of the remnant ("the third" part, cf. 13:8-9) that is brought through the refiner's fire to become the Lord's people.

As announced in 12:4-9, Yahweh will turn Jerusalem's defeat into victory. Although the early church Fathers interpreted the text to mean that Yahweh fights against Jerusalem, the immediate context, parallel passage in 12:1-9, and Hebrew syntax suggest just the opposite. Yahweh the Warrior (Ex. 15:3) will intervene in Israel's behalf *against* the attacking nations. The expression "as when He fights on a day of battle" (v. 3), alludes to Yahweh's intervention in behalf of Israel at the crossing of the Red ("Reed") Sea, when He caused the chariots to swerve and then engulfed the Egyptians in the sea (Ex. 14:13-30). The victory was the Lord's. The people of Israel just stood by and watched God's deliverance.

Having introduced the subject of Yahweh's intervention for His defeated people (14:1-3), Zechariah now provides further details of how that will come about. The Lord will come suddenly from heaven and appear on the Mount of Olives, just east of Jerusalem. The reference to "His feet" may simply be a strong anthropomorphism emphasizing God's personal presence (cf. Ex. 33:18-23), or it may refer to the physical feet of the resurrected Messiah. Jesus' ascension from the Mount of Olives and the promise of His return in like manner (Acts 1:11) point to the latter view. Interpreting verse 4 in this manner is in keeping with the words of 12:10, "They will look upon Me [Jesus, the Messiah] whom they have pierced," a prophecy linked contextually to Jerusalem's deliverance (cf. 12:1-9). Verse 4, then, refers to that great doctrine held so dearly by the church through the ages—the second coming of Jesus to deliver His people, judge the nations, and establish His kingdom (Matt. 24:27-31).

The "Mount of Olives," mentioned only here by that name

but referred to elsewhere (2 Sam. 15:30; 1 Kings 11:7; Ezek. 11:23), is really a mountain ridge that runs north-south and is separated from the city of Jerusalem by the Kidron valley. The Mount of Olives, which receives its name from the numerous olive trees that once grew on its steep slopes, is 2,700 feet in elevation and just east of Jerusalem.

Zechariah declares that on the day of Messiah's return the Mount of Olives will be split from the east to the west by a very large valley. This significant change in topography is the first of a number of changes that will alter the contours of the land of Israel in the eschatological future (cf. 14:10; Ezek. 47). So great will the cleavage be that the mountain will be divided into northern and southern sections. The purpose of the deep valley running east and west between the two sections is revealed in the next verse.

In verse 5 the Lord reveals that the valley opened up through the Mount of Olives at Christ's return will provide an escape route for the besieged and defeated people of Jerusalem. God announces, "And you will flee by the valley of My mountains." The "mountains" (plural) have been taken to refer to the Mount of Olives and the Temple mount, perhaps affected by the cleavage of Olivet. More likely, the "mountains" refer to the northern and southern sections of the Mount of Olives divided by the newly formed valley. The valley for departure is said to "reach to Azel." Azel has not been identified but must be somewhere in the desert east of Jerusalem. The site marks the eastern end of the newly formed valley.

The future departure of the surviving remnant from Jerusalem is compared to the past flight from the city at the time of the great earthquake in the days of Uzziah. That earthquake must have been a memorable one, for Amos dates his prophecy by it (Amos 1:1), and Josephus provides a detailed account of the destruction that followed (Josephus *Antiquities* IX. 225). Zechariah's words "before the earthquake" mean "before the destruction caused by the earthquake." According to Josephus, it occurred when Uzziah went into the

Temple to offer incense (2 Chron. 26:16-21). As the people fled for their lives in anticipation of the collapse of the city, so the future remnant of Jerusalem will flee for safety between the northern and southern sections of the Mount of Olives.

With the safe departure of the remnant from Jerusalem, the Lord will deal out judgment on the attackers of His people. Caught up in the prophetic revelation himself, Zechariah declares, "Then the LORD, my God, will come, and all the holy ones with Him!" (14:5). The "holy ones" refer to the angels or heavenly attendants (Ps. 89:5, 7) who will accompany Christ at His second coming (Mark 8:38; 2 Thess. 1:7; cf. Joel 3:11; Matt. 24:31). The "armies which are in heaven" (Rev. 19:14) will assist the returning Christ in executing judgment on the nations that have attacked Jerusalem. Instead of "with Him" (NASB, following the Septuagint) the Hebrew text reads "with Thee." The change from third to second person may be unexpected for the reader, but is not uncommon in the prophets. Very much involved with the visions they describe, the prophets sometimes address those involved. In animated Hebrew style, Zechariah addresses the Messiah, whose coming he had just described.

The second coming of the Messiah is associated in verse 6 with cosmic upheavel. Zechariah declares, "And it will come about in that day that there will be no light; the luminaries will dwindle." The imagery of darkness as a portent of judgment is common in the prophets (Isa. 5:30; 8:22; 13:9-10; Jer. 32:7-8; Amos 5:18, 20; Zeph. 1:14-15; cf. Matt. 27:45). According to biblical prophecy, the bright glory of Messiah's kingdom must be preceded by the darkness of Tribulation judgment (Isa. 24:23; 60:2; Joel 2:30-32; 3:15; Matt. 24:29-30; Rev. 6:12-13; 8:12). The word "luminaries" (literally, "splended ones") is used in Job 31:26 to denote the radiant splendor of the moon. Here, too, it refers to the heavenly light sources.

The words "will dwindle" represent the *Kethiv* ("that which is *written*") in the Masoretic text whereas the marginal reading of the NASB, "will congeal," represents the *Kere* ("that which is *read*"). Although the *Kethiv* is preferred, either way, the last phrase provides a poetic metaphor emphasizing the fact that there will be "no light."

The uniqueness of the celestial situation is highlighted in verse 7. During this unprecedented period there will be neither day nor night. This has been taken by some to refer to a lengthy period of twilight. On the other hand, it may simply refer to the fact that this period will not be like ordinary days when light and darkness alternate with the earth's rotation. Since the light sources "will dwindle" (14:6), darkness will result. But then the gloom of darkness will be dispelled by the Messiah's glory as Jesus, the Light of the world, returns as promised. The phrase "at evening time" may be understood metaphorically to refer to the end of this period of darkness and judgment. It could also be interpreted quite literally to refer to the evening of a twenty-four hour day when darkness usually falls. Either way, there will be light instead of darkness. This word of hope will undoubtedly be of great encouragement to those enduring the dismal gloom and unprecedented judgment of this period.

The Kingdom of Messiah (14:8-11)

Verses 8-11 describe the culmination of the prophetic promise of a kingdom in which Israel's Messiah rules on David's throne (2 Sam. 7:12-16; cf. Luke 1:31-33). The theme of this section is found in verse 9, "And the LORD will be king over all the earth."

Verse 8 describes how Jerusalem will be a source of perennial streams that will water the whole land. "Living waters" is used in the Old Testament to refer to water that is flowing in contrast to that which is still and stagnant. A spring flows with "living water," whereas a cistern holds stagnant water (cf. Jer. 2:13). Jesus used the imagery of "living water" to refer to the spiritual refreshment available in His Person and through the Holy Spirit (John 4:10, 14; 7:38-39). Half the river will proceed from Jerusalem toward the "eastern sea" (the Salt, or Dead, Sea). The other half will flow toward the "western sea" (the Mediterranean). In contrast with the wadis that fill with water only during Israel's rainy season (November-April), these streams will irrigate the land year-round. An abundance of water for agricultural pursuits is a major characteristic of the Messiah's future kingdom (Isa. 35:6; Joel 3:18).

According to Ezekiel 47:1-12, during Messiah's kingdom a stream will flow from the Temple of God in Jerusalem toward the east. This stream will freshen the salt waters of the Dead Sea and provide for the irrigation of fruit trees that line its banks. It may be that Ezekiel describes the same stream as mentioned by Zechariah but focuses on its eastern branch only. Another stream flowing from "the throne of God and of the Lamb" is described by the apostle John as he relates conditions of the eternal state (Rev. 22:1-2). These life-giving streams all seem to point the reader back to Genesis 2:9-10, which describes a river flowing from Eden. In the kingdom and the eternal state, God's order before the Fall is renewed. The "river of God" motif emphasizes the fact that the blessings of God's people have their source in His Person (cf. Ps. 46:4).

Verse 9 describes a future day when the Lord reestablishes His kingdom on the sphere in which it was challenged by Satan. The "prince of the power of the air" (Eph. 2:2) will be bound in the abyss (Rev. 20:1-3), and Christ will rule supreme as "king over all the earth." His sovereign reign over the earth will fulfill the expectation of the psalmist, who declared by prophetic vision, "The LORD reigns" (Pss. 93:1; 97:1; 99:1). In that day the Messiah will be acknowledged as the one true God. The phrase "the LORD will be one" speaks of both His unity and His uniqueness (cf. Deut. 6:4). His memorial name "Yahweh" ("I AM WHO I AM"; Ex. 3:13-15) will be known and acknowledged as that which represents the one true and living God.

Verse 10 describes the topographical changes that will take place in the land of Israel coincident with Messiah's second coming and the establishment of His kingdom. The moun-

tainous hill country of Judah will be "changed into a plain
from Geba to Rimmon south of Jerusalem." Geba marked
the northern border of Judah during the United Monarchy
(2 Kings 23:8) and is situated about six miles northeast of
Jerusalem at the modern village of Jeba. Rimmon, also
known as En-rimmon (Neh. 11:29; cf. Josh. 15:32) is identified with Khirbet er-Ramamin, about thirty-five miles
southwest of Jerusalem. While the surrounding terrain will be
leveled, Jerusalem itself will be elevated so that the city will
dominate the land (cf. Isa. 2:2; Micah 4:1).

The rest of verse 10 refers to some of the landmarks around
Jerusalem at the time of the restoration. "Benjamin's Gate"
(cf. Jer. 37:12-13) probably refers to a gate in the north wall
of the city. The "First Gate" has not been identified. The
"Corner Gate" (cf. 2 Kings 14:13; Jer. 31:38) appears to have
marked the northwest limit of the city. The "Tower of
Hananel" (Neh. 3:1; 12:39) was a defensive fortification on
the northern wall of Jerusalem. The "king's wine presses"
were situated at the southern extremity of the city near the
King's Pool (Neh. 2:14) and the King's Garden (Neh. 3:15).
The naming of those landmarks emphasized the fact that the
whole city of Jersualem will be elevated to prominence.

Unlike the time of Nehemiah, when the population of
Jerusalem was sparse (Neh. 7:4; 11:1), in the kingdom of
Messiah Jerusalem will be inhabited, and its citizens will dwell
in security. Living under the watchful eye and protective care
of their divine King, the people will enjoy unprecedented
peace and safety (cf. Jer. 23:6; 32:37; 36:16; Ezek. 28:25-26).
The peace and security of Jerusalem is traced to the fact that
there will be "no more curse" (14:11). The word *curse*
(*herem*) is used in the conquest narratives with reference to
cities that were "devoted to complete destruction" (Josh.
6:17, 18; 8:26; 10:28). No longer will military powers rise up
to pursue the destruction of God's people Israel apart from
the intervention of Messiah's rod of iron and the execution of
His righteous judgment (Isa. 2:2-4; Micah 4:2-5; Rev. 19:15).

The promise of "no more curse" appears to have theological as well as military significance. Zechariah anticipates the reversal of the "curse" pronounced on the earth and mankind at the Fall (Gen. 3:14-19). In his description of the eternal state, the apostle John declares, "And there shall no longer be any curse" (Rev. 22:3). This promise looks to the culmination of God's great plan for the ages—to redeem man, reestablish His kingdom authority on earth, and reverse the effects of the Fall.

THE JUDGMENT ON ISRAEL'S ENEMIES (14:12-15)

Verses 12-15 elucidate two previous passages, 12:4-9 and 14:3, and provide further details of how God will fight against and destroy those nations that come up against Jerusalem (cf. Rev. 19:11-16). God promised Abraham that those who cursed his descendants would be cursed (Gen. 12:3). This passage illustrates the outworking of that promise on those nations that have gone to war against Jerusalem.

In verse 12 Zechariah describes the plague that will fall upon those nations that have attacked Jerusalem. The word *plague* is the same one used in Exodus 9:2 with reference to the judgments of God upon the Egyptians. With graphic and rather gruesome detail, Zechariah describes the enemies of Israel as rotting and wasting away. The physical decay of their flesh will take place "while they stand on their feet"—an indication of the rapidity with which the plague will do its work.

According to verse 13 the plague will be accompanied by "great panic," which the Lord brings about among the people (12:4). As God confounded Israel's foes in the past (Judg. 7:22; 1 Sam. 14:20; 2 Chron. 20:23), so He will do in the future. The weapons the enemy intended to use against the Jews they will turn against each other.

Verse 14 records that Judah will join in the fight *at* (not *against*) Jerusalem (cf. 12:5-6). Then as the attackers are destroyed by panic and plague, the people of Judah will join the citizens of Jerusalem in recovering the spoil taken by the enemy (14:1). It appears that they will capture additional booty as well—"gold and silver and garments in great abundance." The enrichment of Jerusalem by the surrounding nations was anticipated by Zechariah's colleague Haggai (Hag. 2:7-8).

In verse 15 Zechariah calls attention to the fact that the plague that falls on Israel's attackers will affect their animals as well. The horses, mules, camels, donkeys, and all the cattle will be destroyed. The extent of the devastation brought on Jerusalem's attackers illustrates the severity of God's judgment upon those who would dare to touch "the apple of His eye" (2:8).

THE WORSHIP IN MESSIAH'S KINGDOM (14:16-21)

The last section of Zechariah 14 describes the worship of "the King, the LORD of hosts" (v. 16) by all the nations. This passage corresponds to 8:20-23, which speaks of the people of the nations going to Jerusalem with Jewish pilgrims to worship the Lord. Having executed judgment on the wicked nations, Messiah the King takes the throne of David to rule the earth and receive the worship of His people.

One would not expect there to be survivors after such a holocaust as described in 14:12-15. But Zechariah gives the impression that there may be. Certainly this is evidence of God's gracious dealings with those who deserve His wrath (2 Pet. 3:9). Zechariah declares in verse 16 that "any who are left of all the nations that went against Jerusalem will go up from year to year to worship the King, the LORD of hosts, and to celebrate the Feast of Booths." Despite their mistreatment of Israel, the repentant will be spared and provided opportunity for regular worship.

The feast of Booths (Tabernacles) was one of Israel's three great pilgrim feasts observed annually by the people of Israel (Deut. 16:13-16). The feast commemorates the wilderness experience of Israel and celebrates the fall harvest (Lev. 23:39, 42-43). It has been suggested that the feast of Tabernacles is mentioned here because as a fall harvest festival it anticipates the gathering of the nations into the kingdom of God.

Verses 17-19 reveal that the worship by the nations of Messiah the King will be strictly enforced. A refusal to participate in worship will result in drought—"There will be no rain" (14:17). The cessation of rainfall, referred to in verse 18 as "the plague with which the LORD smites the nations," was one of the methods used by God in the Old Testament to discipline His apostate people and drive them to repentance (Lev. 26:19-20; Deut. 11:17; 28:24; 1 Kings 17:1; Hag. 1:11).

Egypt is particularly singled out in verses 17 and 18 as being accountable for worship and subject to judgment if that duty is neglected. Why Egypt? Unlike many other nations, Egypt is gifted with a fairly secure water supply. The Nile River provides water for the people of Egypt making them less dependent on seasonal rains. Perhaps the Lord is saying, "Not even Egypt with her secure water supply is immune to the drought I will bring upon those nations that refuse to join in worship." The Lord could stop the torrential rains that feed the Nile in the mountains of equatorial Africa as easily as He could stop the rainful over Israel. Viewed that way, the reference to Egypt would be a warning against any nation thinking it might avoid the divine judgment of drought. On the other hand, it is possible that the reference to Egypt may reflect something of the traditional conflict between the descendants of Abraham by Sarah and his descendants by Hagar (Gen. 16). Again, the emphasis is on the certain judgment to fall on any nation prone to ignore the worship requirements of Messiah's kingdom. In verse 19 the word *punishment* literally reads "sin." However, it speaks in this context of the consequences, or effects, of sin (i.e., "punishment").

Verses 20 and 21 bring Zechariah's prophecy to a close by emphasizing the holiness of the people of God during the kingdom rule of Christ. The high priest of Israel had the words "HOLY TO THE LORD" engraved on the gold headband he wore as he carried out his priestly duties (Ex. 28:36). Zechariah declares that in the kingdom even the bells or tinkling ornaments on the harnesses of horses will bear that inscription. Certainly if the horses are "holy to the LORD," so also will be the people. In that day Israel will realize God's expectation that they be "a kingdom of priests and a holy nation" (cf. Ex. 19:6).

Furthermore, "the cooking pots in the LORD's house will be like the bowls before the altar." No longer will there be a distinction between the secular and the sacred. In the kingdom, even the lowly cooking pot will be sanctified. Others suggest that the point here is that the worshipers will be so numerous that even cooking pots will have to be appropriated for Temple worship. But the emphasis on desecularization seems clear in verse 21, "And every cooking pot in Jerusalem and in Judah will be holy to the LORD of hosts." It is said that the cooking pots will be "holy," not simply that they will be used for Temple ritual.

Zechariah concludes his prophecy with a somewhat enigmatic statement. "And there will no longer be a Canaanite in the house of the LORD of hosts in that day." Since the Canaanites were particularly noted for their expertise as merchants and traders, the term is sometimes used of merchandisers rather than simply in an ethnic sense (Job 41:6; Prov. 31:24).[8] The verse apparently reflects the practice of Canaanite merchants frequenting the Temple courts with their wares (cf. Matt. 21:12; John 2:14). During his second governorship, Nehemiah had to deal with the problem of such merchants entering Jerusalem to sell their goods on the Sabbath (Neh. 13:19-22). In view of the sanctity of all the bowls and pots in the kingdom age, no longer will there be potential customers for those wares at the Temple area. The phrase suggests that the unclean and the godless, such as those who would disregard the sanctity of the Temple, will have no place in the future kingdom.[9] The bells, pots, and people of the kingdom will be "holy to the LORD."

8. B. Maisler, "Canaan and the Canaanites," *Bulletin of the American Schools of Oriental Research* 102 (April 1946): 10-12.

9. David Baron, *The Visions and Prophecies of Zechariah* (London: Marshall, Morgan & Scott, 1918), p. 532.

CONCLUSION

Zechariah's name means "Yahweh remembers." Throughout his prophecy that truth is confirmed and illustrated. The God of Israel has not forgotten His covenant people. Although He has had to discipline His people for their apostasy and unbelief, His purpose has always been to draw them to repentance. On the basis of Israel's repentance and spiritual renewal, the Lord will bring to full realization the promises He has given His people.

The message of Zechariah is beautifully highlighted in Isaiah 49:14-15. Disheartened by the discipline of exile, Zion declares, "The LORD has forsaken me, and the LORD has forgotten me." God Himself responds with an illustration and a promise. "Can a woman forget her nursing child, and have no compassion on the son of her womb?" As awful as it is, mothers sometimes neglect and even abuse their own children. Then the Lord adds a promise that has given His people grounds for confidence and encouragement through the ages. "Even these may forget, but I will not forget you."

APPENDIX

The book of Zechariah has been thought by some to be a difficult book to preach or teach. Somewhat intimidated by its unusual visions and enigmatic prophecies, some preachers, Sunday school teachers, and Bible-study leaders have for all practical purposes neglected the significant and very practical messages of the book. These homiletical suggestions are designed to assist Christian workers using Zechariah in their ministries. Only when Zechariah is studied, personally applied, and shared with others will we with the apostle Paul be declaring the "whole counsel of God" (Acts 20:27).

1:1	A biographical sketch of Zechariah, "God remembers."
1:2-6	A call to repentance. Verse 3, "Do not be like your fathers," makes an intriguing Father's Day message.
1:7—6:15	An eight-week period of Zechariah's night visions.
1:7-17	Israel is in the news. God has promised to bless His people.
1:18-21	Here comes the Judge! God is sovereign. He will overthrow oppressive and wicked nations.
2:1-13	Jerusalem's future hope. God has promised to protect His people by His personal presence.
3:1-10	God provides cleansing from sin through Jesus, the Messiah.

4:1-14   Moving mountains God's way. Depend on God's power, not on human ingenuity.

5:1-4   Be sure your sin will find you out. God's great love does not preclude the exercise of His wrath in judgment.

5:5-11   Spiritual spot remover. God's removal of iniquity and wickedness from the land.

6:1-8   Judgment begins at the UN. God will execute judgment on the nations.

6:9-15   The making of Messiah's crown jewels. In the future kingdom the Messiah will fill the offices of king and priest.

7-8   Focusing on worship; devote several studies to the priority of true worship. What does God require?

7:1-7   God's view of empty ritual. Worship must be God-centered rather than man-centered.

7:8-14   God's requirement of practical righteousness. Worship is not just a Sunday morning spectator activity.

8:1-17   Obligations of great blessing. God's goodness to us ought to encourage kindness in our dealings with others.

8:18-23   Worship in the kingdom. In the future kingdom, fasts will become feasts in view of God's personal presence among His people.

9-14   Christ in prophecy. This section of Zechariah is well-suited for a series of studies of what the Old Testament teaches concerning the first and second coming of Christ.

9:1-10   Here comes Jesus! His first coming as a suffering Savior and His second coming as a reigning King.

9:11-17   Deliverance through Messiah's coming. Israel's future and hope (Romans 11).

10:1-12   Blessings of Messiah's coming. By way of ap-

	plication, focus on the believer's "blessed hope" (Titus 2:13).
11:1-17	"But His own did not receive Him" (John 1:11). The Good Shepherd is rejected by His people.
12:1-9	A mighty fortress is our God! Jerusalem's physical deliverance at Christ's coming.
12:10—13:1	Israel's saddest day. Israel's realization that they crucified Jesus, their Messiah.
13:2-6	God, the zodiac, and palm readers. God's dealings with false prophets.
13:7-9	Israel in the refiner's fire. God's dealings with His people in light of Messiah's rejection.
14:1-7	Messiah's re-entry. Jesus is coming again to judge the nations and establish His kingdom.
14:8-11	Paradise regained. King Jesus reigns over His kingdom.
14:12-15	The world's end: nuclear holocaust or divine wrath? God's judgment executed on the nations that have persecuted Israel.
14:16-21	Worship: an option or an obligation. Worshiping the King in His kingdom.

For further help in preaching or teaching the message of Zechariah consult Walter C. Kaiser, *Toward an Exegetical Theology: Biblical Exegesis for Preaching and Teaching* (Grand Rapids: Baker, 1981).

SELECTED BIBLIOGRAPHY

Baldwin, Joyce G. *Haggai, Zechariah, Malachi*. Tyndale Old Testament Commentaries. London: Inter-Varsity, 1972.

Baron, David. *The Visions and Prophecies of Zechariah*. London: Marshall, Morgan & Scott, 1918.

Cashdan, Eli. "Zechariah." In *The Twelve Prophets,* pp. 267-332. Edited by A. Cohen. London: Soncino, 1948.

Feinberg, Charles L. *God Remembers: A Study of Zechariah,* 4th ed. Portland, Oregon: Multnomah, 1965.

———. *The Minor Prophets*. Moody Press combined edition. Chicago: Moody, 1976.

Leupold, H. C. *Exposition of Zechariah*. Columbus, Ohio: Wartburg, 1965.

Mason, Rex. *The Books of Haggai, Zechariah and Malachi*. The Cambridge Bible Commentary. Cambridge: Cambridge U., 1977.

Meyer, F. B. *The Prophet of Hope*. Chicago: Revell, 1900.

Mitchell, H. G.; Smith, John M. P.; and Bewer, Julius A. *A Critical and Exegetical Commentary on Haggai, Zechariah, Malachi and Jonah*. New York: Scribner's, 1912.

Perowne, T. T. *Haggai and Zechariah*. The Cambridge Bible. Cambridge: Cambridge U., 1886.

Pusey, E. B. *The Minor Prophets*. 2 vols. Grand Rapids: Baker, 1950.

Unger, Merrill F. *Zechariah: Prophet of Messiah's Glory*. Grand Rapids: Zondervan, 1963.

Wright, Charles H. H. *Zechariah and His Prophecies*. London: Hodder and Stroughton, 1879; reprint ed., Minneapolis: Klock & Klock, 1980.